And It Begins

A MEMOIR

And It Begins

A Memoir

by Pudu Blamoh

and Linda Fitzpatrick

Foreword by

Abigail E. Disney

and Leymah Gbowee

Contents

Foreword

High school is hard. Being a teenager is hard. But high school and your teen years are especially hard when you are far from home and family, feeling challenged in the most fundamental ways, wondering who you are and what you were put on this earth to do—all while navigating a wholly foreign social environment you suspect might just be the least hospitable one you've ever encountered.

Pudu and Linda are in some ways typical for their ages and circumstances, special in others. They faced all these challenges and more while making their way through those four tough years on their way to college. And we are very lucky that they want to share all they've learned with us.

It is immediately obvious to both them and to their readers that they could not have come from more different circumstances. What is remarkable is how quickly they come to see that their differences are dwarfed by all that they share in common. And because they face their respective challenges with such resolution and integrity, it is easy to see why they become fast friends in spite of all the reasons they had to have nothing to share with one another.

This book is a story—both together and separate—of two girls making their way through challenges and fears with a powerful friendship to buoy them up. It is a story of lessons learned, character built and dreams discovered.

I am so proud of what Pudu and Linda have to say about their lives in friendship and I think you will learn a lot about them, and about yourself in reading their book.

ABIGAIL E. DISNEY

Foreword

And It Begins is a refreshing story of hope and friendship, especially in a world where the rhetoric globally is "Us vs. Them." Linda and Pudu's journey is a testament that seeds of peace planted in young children can definitely lead to postive change and good examples.

Pudu and Linda are showing not just young people but adults alike that we must and should always interact on the basis of our common humanity. They teach us through their friendship to constantly move past race, class, religion and social status and ask, "I see your humanity, do you see mine?"

To say I am proud of these two outstanding young ladies would be an understatement.

LEYMAH GBOWEE

The first day we met at Proctor Academy.

PREFACE

Linda

Some students have a background, identity, interest, or talent that is so meaningful they believe their application would be incomplete without it. If this sounds like you, then please share your story.

"Though I consider myself a storyteller, I rarely tell my own story. I steer away from it out of modesty, privacy, or just mere lack of interest as compared to the characters I create. The time has come for my voice—my own voice, not the voice of my characters—to speak.

I have no intention of painting myself a success story, but truthfully, I have risen above my fair share of challenges in my first eighteen years. Some of these challenges include struggling with health issues, later resolved by two neurosurgeries, as well as learning the skills to manage dyslexia. I have proven that living with "unstoppable determination"—my elementary headmaster's words—goes a long way. But these stories don't prove who I am; they merely demonstrate where I am coming from. Why should you care about my history when you are assessing my future potential? My past sets the groundwork for my future, and while my story begins with challenges, it ends with dreams.

In elementary school, my parents were afraid to let me sign up for the school play. They were concerned that memorizing lines would be too difficult. However, when I performed in my first play, my world opened to a whole new form of expression. Memorizing lines became a hobby, and I even performed the entire play for my babysitter so many times that I no longer needed the script. Acting, as a form of storytelling, gave me the confidence to explore characters, and myself, in new ways. When writing, I fully immerse myself in the creative process and, through my characters, explore a range of thoughts, dreams, and desires. Both performing and writing have allowed me to express multiple sides of my personality. For instance, in eighth grade we were instructed to create a character—mine was an emotional teenage male popstar. I was then paired with another classmate to perform a scene. One of the most daring performances in my class, I donned a blonde "Bieber" wig and baggy pants, getting into character so much that people were astonished to discover the actress behind the scene. This love for performance and storytelling led me to write, direct, and produce my own play at camp this past summer. The most gratifying part of the experience was not the welcome reaction of the audience, but the positive impact my script had on the young cast.

As a Freshman, I attended Proctor Academy where I met one of my closest friends. Pudu is from Africa, raised in Liberia and Ghana, and she has taught me just how much strength and love can come from having a friend who is more like family. We met when we were both new to everything: high school, New Hampshire, and each other. Our lives are almost polar opposites; that is what makes our relationship so mean-ingful. Through thick and thin, this friendship has filled me with gratitude and an eagerness to explore the world and its cultures. I believe we cannot tell stories until we learn to incor-porate and appreciate everyone's language—not the words they speak, but the message behind them. In this friend, I have begun to discover this aspect of storytelling.

I hope I have enlightened you with snapshots into my identity. It is hard to say what will matter of my history down the road, but these peeks into my life capture the eighteen-year old spirit today—of a dreamer with a future on her horizon in creative writing. I look forward to greeting any chal-lenges that lie ahead and further developing my voice. For now, I will continue to write the stories my characters breathe within."

I think this essay is one of the most honest reflections of myself in recent years and it highlights the very things that are most important to me—courage, storytelling, and friendship.

I also think it is important to further emphasize the purpose of *And it Begins*. It is by no means to "paint myself a success story." I am not perfect, and neither is Pudu. Our high school journeys are completely individual to us. So whatever age you are, your high school experience doesn't need to compare to ours—in fact, it shouldn't, and I sincerely hope it doesn't. Live and reflect on your life as you please. This is ours.

And who are we anyway?

We are just two storytellers trying to find meaning behind the last 1,460 days of our lives. We are just two teenagers from incredibly different backgrounds trying to bring a greater purpose to our friendship. We are at the beginning of our entire lives and we couldn't be more excited to see our dreams turn to reality.

Standing in my empty dorm room at the end of freshman year. It's still incredible to me how quickly time passes.

CHAPTER ONE

Orientation

Linda

The ride up to New London, New Hampshire was long and sickening. I was one hundred percent positive that Proctor Academy was the school for me, but the daunting idea of having to spend a weekend in the woods the next day with complete strangers weighed on my mind. And the fact that I would be living for an entire year with someone originally from another country. Living away from home wasn't what bothered me. I knew I could. I'd already been to summer camp for four years—seven weeks without technology was harder than this. But, God, was I nervous.

Something happened when I first met Pudu, who I knew as Princess Blamoh. My parents and I parked outside my dorm located right off a busy highway street at the start of campus. I had no idea what to expect of Pudu. We only corresponded once in late August. This is the exact message Pudu sent me after a few weeks delay.

"Hi Linda,

This is Princess or Pudu your new roommate. Sorry I couldn't get back to you earlier, you sent the email to my mom's mail and she just told me. I don't really know what to say in messages like this but I guess I will just tell you a bit about me.

Since we are going to be sharing rooms you should know that I am a bit messy so, if you are a neat freak you are probably going to be breathing down my neck a lot. I'm hoping you are not."

I can recall the exact moment I opened that email. I was with my mother in her black Mazda CX 9, which is now my car. I got a rushing sense of calmness reading about

Pdu's lack of cleanliness. Not because I liked the fact that she didn't clean up her stuff, but because it was such a genuine response. That quickly became one of my favorite qualities about Pudu. She tells you the truth, and she does it kindly.

So, there I am, nervous as hell and sick to my stomach as I open the front door of my dorm with only the knowledge that my new roommate is messy. She was sitting in the common room just to the left of the entrance. I could see her kneeling down trying to charge her phone. She wore a purple t-shirt and had her hair in braids. She immediately jumped up and greeted me, as if she'd been waiting for her new friend. Up in the room, she'd already settled herself in and helped my mother and I unpack. She could talk, which was good considering my emotional state. Even though many of the stories she was telling where so different than the experiences I had lived through (war, separation from her mother, moving to a new country), I knew that I was going to be okay the moment she mentioned writing. Writing first became a passion of mine in seventh grade, so here I was two years later, working on a novel and delighted to know that, no matter what, we could share the common interest of stories. It's a pivotal component of our friendship. Pudu is the only friend I have who understands the depths at which creating stories and characters take. She gives some of the best advice I have heard. And she is willing to read even the roughest drafts while making an effort to point out the work's better qualities along with its weak moments. That's invaluable to me.

Later on, after beginning to feel comfortable at this new boarding school, my dorm parent came around ushering my parents away. I think everybody has had a moment like this, where suddenly you realize your world is about to spin around again. I could feel it in my stomach. The moment was here.

I walked to Jake's, the gas station and convenience store across the street, with my parents before they drove off. I got sick. I cried. And then I said goodbye like a brave fourteen year old. My mother still remarks that she was amazed that, no matter how nervous I was, I never questioned staying. I didn't ask my parents to take me home with them or try to make an excuse for them to stay longer. I knew with no uncertainty that Proctor Academy was the place for me. I was willing to fight the tears in order to enjoy future smiles.

*　　*　　*

You never notice how loud trucks are until they're speeding along the highway outside your bedroom window at three in the morning. I rolled around in bed my first night at Proctor listening to the new norms of my surroundings. The rumble of logs on the back of a delivery truck. The short lived silence. The zoom of rubber wheels burning up the pavement below. The crinkle of Pudu's blanket as she turns in bed. The mumble of a singer's voice and rock drums seeping out of a truck driv-er's window until my mind drifts off to sleep again.

The lack of these noises early in the morning wouldn't have let me sleep any more than I did. My nerves were too active at the thought of heading out on orientation. Five days hiking was not my kind of fun. I lay awake in bed early, sick to my stomach again, trying to distract myself with a text to my mother and a few friends from summer camp. I know I said something along the lines of, "If I don't make it back alive, I love you." Pudu and I didn't talk much this morning, but I know she could tell how nervous I was. She's since said so.

Orientation wasn't as bad as I expected. We hiked up and down a mountain, attempted to learn how to build a tent (which I never quite mastered), and experienced a weekend in the woods unique to us all. Once we were on top of the mountain, we gathered on the rocky surface to stargaze. I re-member having a conversation with another freshman about *Rollie Pollie Ollie* and childhood television shows. The future seemed so bright.

Then, on the last night, we got caught in a storm, which freaked my parents out, who were back in Marblehead safely inside. My mother called my advisor and tracked the storm, panicked because she knew I was most likely in it. I was. I was in the heart of it. But I was oblivious to this fact and her concern, lying in a wet tent, talking quietly with others under the rumble of thunder and flashes of lighting. I guess you could say that's pretty much what being an adolescent is. Managing to live a life around chaos and confusion, both enjoying and fearing the madness and uncertainty of it all.

*   *   *

Just a couple months into school, my life suddenly changed once again. I received a severe concussion after being hit by a soccer ball during warm ups for a game one Saturday morning. I played the entirety of the game, aggressively because I wanted to impress my parents who had come to watch. After dinner, I fell asleep for a few hours and woke up feeling awful—looking like it, too. Monday morning I went to the trainers and was officially diagnosed with a concussion. I was told to spend my afternoons, when I would usually be at soccer practice or games, in my room resting.

But these afternoons became months and the next thing I know four years have passed and I still have Post Concussion Syndrome. Headaches have become a steady part of my life, after having never dealt with them before.

This concussion isolated me from the prime form of social interaction at Proctor. I was forced to spend more time than I wanted in my room. I was sent home before final exams because I was too sick to take them. Everything was a little out of place.

Almost as out of place as I felt later in the year when my closest friend, aside from Pudu, was hit by a car while talking on the phone with me.

I'll never forget that night. My friend and I were going to a study session together, so she was calling to let me know she was ready to go. As she was walking across the highway street in front of my dorm, a car pulled out from the parking lot and didn't see her. Luckily, she wasn't badly hurt at all, just a few bruises. But I remember looking out my window after hearing a scream trying to determine what was happening. It didn't immediately occur to me that my friend was in danger, because I saw a car near a pole and I figured that was the accident, but when I received no response on the other end of the phone, I got worried.

Pudu was in the room next door with some friends. I wanted to go in and ask if they knew what was going on, but it took me a while to summon the courage to do so. That's something that never really stuck out to me until now, looking back. I was so shy that even walking into a room full of my friends was scary. That shouldn't have been the case. Yes, it was the beginning of my freshman year and I was still in the process of meeting people, but I should have felt more comfortable than I actually did.

I don't know why I was suddenly so shy. Maybe it was the stress of the situation that kept me lingering in my room—maybe I was subconsciously scared about the news I would hear. I don't know. All I know is that this clearly shows I wasn't completely comfortable at Proctor.

If I had not become concussed, I may never have realized the lack of activities at Proctor. And maybe that would have been fine. Maybe sports would have been enough. If my friend hadn't walked across that street at that time, maybe I would never have realized how shy I could be or the lack of security I had around those friends. Maybe freshman year excitement wouldn't have revolved around car crashes and head injuries. Maybe I would have found a way to live at Proctor, but we can't reverse history. I wouldn't want to either. The fact of the matter is, Proctor Academy was trying hard to be the place I wanted it to be, but it so clearly wasn't. But, of course, I didn't think any of this in the reality of either moment.

CHAPTER TWO

Powerless

Pudu

It's not easy to talk about my freshman year of high school. It was greatly intimidating, grossly overwhelming, and incredibly beneficial to the person I am today. I found out I was coming to Proctor somewhere around April. I was super excited; I screamed for about five minutes. I had what seemed like a long time to prepare for my departure, an entire summer to say goodbye to my friends. What I didn't realize was I never really got to say goodbye because I spent the summer in France with my cousins.

For the first time since I had given up my tomboy badge for boys, I was in a different country, with different customs. I was allowed to wear a bikini without feeling singled out and I was excited and scared, and decided that it was time to shave my legs.

Baby Pudu 2007 in Monrovia.

My leg hair up until eighth grade was my pride and joy —leg hair, back hair, any kind of hair is beauty where I come from. I came to realize that was not the case in either France or America. So, here I was, fourteen years old, and I'm getting rid of parts of myself that I had spent most of my life being proud of. I believe this summer was the disintegration of Princess and the beginning of Pudu.

I picked Pudu as the name to be called in school because it said in the brochure that nicknames were allowed at Proctor, so if everyone was doing it, why shouldn't I? I didn't take into account the fact that I had never really been Pudu without my mother, my siblings and my close relatives. Pudu had never existed outside of my Ghanaian home and its Liberian counterpart.

Pudu was the outspoken little girl who jumped out of trees onto plastic chairs. Pudu had never been anywhere besides at home and with family.

I don't know if picking a different name would have made a difference, but I would like to believe I picked Pudu because I needed to know Pudu.

I got to Proctor and jumped in with both feet, and started to swim. Towards what? I still don't know, but I started to swim. The more I swam, the less I recognized, and the less I recognized, the more I began to resist the urge to swim. In the end, I quit swimming and I started to float. During the first few weeks of getting to know people, I fell into this haze and the only time that made sense was when I got back to my dorm room.

I remember Linda and I during the first couple days of school waking up really early and getting ready and walking the short-long distance to the dining hall. I think we both hoped to meet people and find our click, but I'm still not sure. However, we did this for all of three days, I think, before we collectively gave up and resulted having dried cereal or bagels in the morning for breakfast. Meals weren't important to me. The dining hall was stressful—incredibly stressful—freshman year, so much so I kinda deleted it from my memory. In fact, a lot of places at Proctor that I wasn't mandated to be at felt like scary traps to another planet.

Our room became my sanctuary. (This is where I use my great education at Proctor to justify my messiness.) I felt so safe in our room that I just didn't like changing it. I liked it the way it was. When it got too messy, I fought Linda tooth and nail to keep it the way it was—I was also lazy, but that's besides the point.

The point is when I had zombified my way through classes and kicked at a soccer ball for hours in the rain, wind or heat, I got to walk back to our dorm, Ives house, took off my muddy cleats in my room, jumped on my bed, and immersed myself in music. If Linda was asleep, I wore headphones and read. If Linda was away at the trainers, I played it loud and had a dance party. The shades were always closed in those moments, though. Linda's Justin Bieber and One Direction posters were my only audience as I belted Sam Cooke or Fuse ODG. My click freshman year was Linda and sometimes our next door neighbor, but that was another kind of relationship, not particularly healthy in my opinion.

The pushover in me hates to be manipulated. I was the youngest child for eleven years and all I'd ever been was manip-ulated. I can't remember the day I met this friend, that mem-ory is gone, but subsequent memories stay fresh and keep me vigilant. What does one do when the routine set to keep things in motion is disrupted? When you can't do your homework because someone decides to take your laptop? I can't remember if it was fall, winter or spring, but I remember my friend taking my computer one day because I refused to do something for her.

By that time, my computer had become my lifeline. It was my tunnel to the universe where everything was safe and compartmentalized, where I played video games online with my best boyfriend. Her actions screwed with me; she didn't just take my computer, she took my power away from me and the fact that I wasn't able to get it back on my own had me calling Abby, a woman who acts as my second mom, to complain. I was frustrated, annoyed, angry and disappointed. On several occasions when I refused to clean the room Linda would take my computer and place it on her bed until I did. This friend left the room with it that day, and I was powerless to even voice my emotions.

It seems insignificant now that a computer would cause me to call home in panic, and later trek up to my advisor's house with Linda to hash out the situation. It really wasn't fun at the time. Linda and I returned to Ives a few hours later in time for study hall and my friend did give back my computer, but the fact is for one afternoon, I was relegated to the back-seat of my own life. I was being handled and propped up and I felt incapable of standing up for myself. I never wanted to feel that way again.

> I'm different
> Hairy legs are sexy,
> Hairy legs are beautiful,
> Hairy legs means the hair on your head is kicking.
> Let me rephrase that,
> In Liberia and Ghana where I come from,
> Where I was born, then raised,
> Where generations of beautiful brown people have lived, Where I call home, hairy legs are beautiful.

I have one of the hairiest legs I have ever seen on a girl (when left unshaved); they rival my brothers' and when I arrived at Proctor, I didn't see the problem with them. During our wilderness orientation while I was wearing shorts I was unaware I had anything to be conscious of, but when I got back to campus, I looked around and realized everybody looked completely different from me. Every other girl in the room had silky hair that they grew on their own. Other girls were dressed in cute jean shorts and floral dresses. I had on a knee length African print skirt that showed my hairy legs. No one else looked like me. My jokes fell short. I was suddenly arrested by the differences between myself and other students in the room.

That's a moment that broke something in me. My culture was not a part of this place. I was the only person of my cultural heritage; I was the other. I was an oddity and people asked me questions about this place I came from and they had no idea where it was. I was asked the same questions over and over again; I gave the same response until I stopped giving responses at all.

Silence became my best friend; when I wasn't with my best friends, I forgot to speak up, I forgot my voice, I forgot my words. I didn't know how to interact with people anymore, I didn't know how I fit in outside of my room.

CHAPTER THREE

Proctor

Linda

"Is she happy?" Jack asked my mother in the car once, just as Sophomore year was beginning. Perhaps it was his twin telepathy that led him to believe I wasn't happy or maybe I was showing signs of sadness. I can't say, but what I do know is that he was happy. He found his place in a community he dreamed of attending since he was ten years old, after his baseball coach mentioned it. Jack was the leading force convincing our parents to visit and apply to Groton School. His love for the school was perhaps the only reason my parents then let me look at boarding schools.

When March rolled around and decision day was upon us, nobody—besides maybe Jack—thought he would be accepted. Not because we didn't think he was smart or deserved it, but because of the high rigor of the school.

My mother had come up with the idea to bet with candy on every school we each applied to. We had three categories—accepted, waitlisted, or denied—and using M&M's we bet the likelihood of each option.

Jack won every last bit when it came to Groton.

He believed in himself and proved us all happily wrong. Ever since that day Groton School has been the perfect place for him.

I think that's what he wanted for me. Because of boarding school, our bond grew more distant than it ever was. We've never texted much with each other, and being away for months at a time didn't help with our communication. I remember times he would enter my room at home to say goodbye and I would feel this emptiness in my gut, regret maybe, because there wasn't enough time. Even when I was

At Jack's high school graduation.

at Marblehead High, we never seemed to hang out enough.

Jack's my forever friend. He has been protecting me long before I knew I needed a guardian at my back. We somehow just get each other; not necessarily in the way that I always know what he's thinking or that we always want the same things, because we certainly don't at times, but we don't argue and we've never had a reason to.

He knew before I did.

I was sad, though I kept the fact largely to myself. But, see, I wasn't unhappy. I was just trying to be happy, unwilling to give up just yet. Not ready to admit my perfect place wasn't perfect after all.

If I had been in the car that afternoon, I would have said yes. Yes, I was happy. I probably still would, because while Proctor wasn't my home-away-from-home, I wasn't miserable Freshman year. Sophomore year was going to be difficult, I knew that. With Pudu away in Costa Rica for the fall, everything I had grown used to was going to change. But I arrived with a game plan to get involved in more activities and make new friends quickly. While this game plan dissolved quickly, at the time of Jack's question, I wasn't able to admit my honest emotions yet.

A friend of mine from summer camp was transferring to Proctor for Sophomore year, which was exciting. Nobody knows this, but I requested to have her placed in the same dorm as me in hope of helping me branch out, since Pudu would be gone in the fall and I would be in a single dorm room. I was sitting at my kitchen table when my friend texted me about her dorm placement. She wasn't in Davis. I had never told her about the plan, but I remember sitting there thinking, *What is happening?* My mom called Proctor to learn the faculty member in charge of housing had forgotten about his promise to me. He had forgotten.

A few weeks later I moved into my single in Davis, a building that was laid out strangely and didn't foster easy social interactions. My friend was busy with her move in, but we saw each other briefly. Later in the day, once my parents had left, there was a student gathering that I went to. I was hoping my friend would introduce me to the people she had met over orientation, but she was busy assimilating to the culture of Proctor on her own. Maybe if I had told her I wanted to be included more she would have, because she's a really kind person. She just didn't know my situation. We arranged a couple times to go to dinner together, but she forgot and went with other people. This was the beginning of the downward spiral of my happiness at Proctor. Probably unfairly, I put a lot of pressure on the idea of having a friend from elsewhere joining my Proctor community. You know, I didn't expect us to be best friends, but I guess I just hoped she'd pull me into her social crowd. At this point, I don't know if anything would have been different had we been in the same dorm. Yes, it was frustrating to have faculty forget about me and the plans we arranged, but maybe that's what I needed.

*   *   *

I was driving with my father in the car once when he asked me if I liked to read.

"Yeah. I don't do it a lot during the school year, but I read a lot at camp. Why?"

He wanted to know more about dyslexia. He had done his research along with my mother when I was diagnosed, but he wanted to know what it was like. I think everyone does, which is probably why dyslexia is wildly misrepresented in media.

I'm dyslexic. I've grown to be very proud of that. But I recognize that my dyslexia is so different than others. It's a "learning disability" that is unique to each individual, something I love. Because I was diagnosed at the crisp age of four and enrolled in Landmark Elementary Middle School at six, I never had classroom horror stories. Sure, I remember being taken out of my preschool art class for special education classes—something that always irked me because I still remember being unable to finish a Mother's Day card. But, I wasn't faced with my struggle. I knew nothing about dyslexia when I entered Landmark. It was just another school. That has given me a very interesting perspective on dyslexia and Landmark. I certainly know what it's like not to know how to pronounce or mispronounce a word—I probably do that every day—and I misspell words religiously. I lived with the fear of making a mistake and being labeled the dumb, dyslexic girl through middle school. I just haven't had a moment where I was being told there was a mistake and I couldn't see it in a while. It reminds me that we all perceive the world differently. If more people could just remember that, maybe there would be less negativity, less harassment.

With Faith Hall and her daughter Cora. Faith was my fourth grade teacher at Landmark EMS, tutored me in middle school, and along the way became a great friend and woman to look up to. She taught me to advocate for myself and be confident in the person I was becoming. It is because of her and other Landmark teachers that I graduated with honors.

It's very difficult for me to describe living with dyslexia though. I don't know anything different. I'm not looking at a page of swirling letters. I see the words. I recognize them. Sometimes I know what a word is but I can't figure out how to pronounce it out loud, but in my head I know what it sounds like. Other times I simply struggle to determine how the letters combine to create the word. So I sound things out when I'm writing, rely a little heavier on spellcheck. It's nothing monumental to me. Granted this is very much due to the education I received.

My Landmark teachers helped me master incredible skills—everything from organization to advocating for myself. Maybe my life would be very different without everything I learned as an elementary student, but that's not a hypothesis I can test. I like to read. I love to write. I'm not afraid of a little hard work—and, though I'm often working harder than my peers, I don't notice it. That's why it's so hard to describe. I'm dyslexic, but I don't notice.

Freshman year, our entire school sat in the auditorium at Proctor to watch an educational movie about a dyslexic boy. It was supposed to teach the community about dyslexics and the struggles they face. I've never felt so targeted, so uncomfortable and disappointed than I was sitting in that dark theater being forced to watch a movie that I felt completely missed the point of what living with dyslexia really is. The movie was depressing. Sure, the boy found a passion in art, but the film didn't make you believe in him or his future. It was awful and beyond stereotypical. And far worse was how enthusiastic the Proctor teachers were about how fantastic the movie was. The message wasn't positive, despite what they thought. They had no idea what they were talking about. Nobody knew how to handle dyslexia at Proctor, even the learning skills teachers.

One of the great things about Proctor was that it offered a learning skills program that many kids took advantage of. It was basically just a built-in tutoring session in your class schedule.

Before starting school, I attended a Proctor get together. It was held by a family who lived at the end of my old street in Swampscott. The mother had taught me lacrosse as a middle schooler so our families had built a relationship already, which led to honesty. The daughter was at Proctor, maybe a grade ahead of me, and she also went to Landmark. When she was placed into the learning skills program, she was given the same teacher as me.

This teacher had been at Proctor for years. Over and over again, she had been given dyslexic students to work with and over and over again, the pairings didn't work.

My old Landmark friend and I were paired together in the same tutorial session. Things for the first months were okay—far from great, but I hadn't felt the desire to change yet. Until one specific conversation; a mind boggling, anger-inducing conversation.

At the end of a class, our teacher told my friend and I that we were like her son who had a serious physical disability. I mean no offense to anyone with a disability, but to me, dyslexia is the farthest thing from that. But the teacher sat there in front of us with that ignorant smile of hers saying that we were at such a great disadvantage to everyone else, but that she understood us and could help us get through school. Perhaps she had the right intentions, but I was so appalled. Appalled because how could I be expected to learn from somebody who knew nothing about my "disability?" How was I supposed to feel comfortable around a teacher who already saw me as weak and disadvantaged? Things didn't add up; and I was mad that the person who was supposed to be encouraging me was placing boundaries on me.

I remember pacing my dorm room as I called my parents and told them. Pudu was on her bed listening as I retold the conversation.

My parents raised me to believe in no limitations. Nothing about my upbringing was any different than Jack's. As someone who struggled immensely with being labeled dyslexic in middle school, and who at this point had grown to appreciate all that it brought to my life, this whole thing was just heart breaking. The fact that my teacher was the one to hold me back, or trying to, bothered me most. I could handle the insult, but I knew someone out there couldn't. There might be a student who hasn't come to love the fact they're dyslexic yet and if they get placed with this teacher, who treats them with no respect, that could ruin any self-esteem they've built for themselves so far. I didn't like what our teacher had to say, and I switched very quickly to a different learning skills teacher after this conversation, but I could have handled it. I needed to make a statement for somebody who couldn't. I don't know why Proctor kept putting dyslexics with teachers who don't know about teaching to different learning styles, especially after so many failed attempts, but hopefully with my transition, I was sending a signal. Stop trying to force it. Or at least educate your teachers better first.

*   *   *

I always wanted a Sweet 16th birthday party. To me sixteen was this incredible age where you finally got to grow up and that was worth celebrating. But, having a September birthday, I knew heading back to Proctor Sophomore year that this dream would never become a reality. Before Jack and I left for school, we celebrated with family. And before that we celebrated with our grandparents. So, honestly, as September 12th neared, it felt like it had passed long ago. Maybe that was a good thing because my 16th birthday was far from the dream.

On the evening before my birthday, I called my mother, crying heavily because the reality of my situation was finally catching up to me. Proctor Academy just wasn't the place for me. I didn't have many close friends and there was nothing to do besides play sports, which was no longer an option due to the severe concussion I received the previous year. I had tried working with my guidance counselor to meet new people and find other activities, but nothing was available to me. I felt so defeated. Proctor Academy was the school I knew without a doubt I wanted to be at, but…the vision of what it was supposed to be and the reality of what it was were separating vastly.

I can't recall what threw me overboard and made me call my mother. All I remember is walking home from Pizza Chef, with the same friend who was hit by a car the previous year, and going into my dorm. My friend went back to her dorm, which was down the road a bit, and maybe we planned to hang out later. Later never came that particular night. When I got into my stuffy, single dorm room, tucked back on the outskirts of the main campus, I sat at my desk and let the emotions I'd been hiding be acknowledged in a way they hadn't yet been for this situation.

My mom knew right away the seriousness of the call. Both my parents were on the phone with me trying to get a handle on my sudden tears and began to formalize a plan of action. It was hours. It was emotional. It was honest.

We talked pretty much up until I went to bed. I remember them ending the call saying, "Happy Birthday," and feeling a sullen smile creep on my face. This wasn't a celebratory time. And then, I forgot it was my birthday. I woke up, emotionally drained from the evening before, completely unaware of the day until I looked at my phone and saw messages from camp friends. I vividly remember lying in my bed feeling this massive sense of *wow* hovering above me. I never knew I would forget, perhaps, one of the most important days of my life—a day I'd dreamt about celebrating since I was a child.

The day wasn't completely miserable, but it wasn't the dream either.

I shared a cake with my dorm mates. I was friendly with a couple people in the dorm, so it was fun to celebrate with them. Overall, it was a nice evening, but it was too late for nice.

I'll never forget this birthday. In fact, just this year I was in awe at what can happen with time. I spent my 18th in the way I wished I'd spent my 16th—at a concert with good friends.

I remember standing in Gillette Stadium, watching the sea of white lights sway to the music, and looking at a Marblehead High School friend and a middle school friend thinking, I'm happy. We don't get a real say in what happens to us, and sometimes that is really difficult to come to terms with, but I do believe everything happens for a reason. Sometimes the reasons are obvious, and sometimes they take two years to present themselves.

One Direction concert on my 18th birthday.

CHAPTER FOUR
Little Things, Tomatoes

Pudu

"Yo no hablo espanol. Solo pocito."

Truer words had not been spoken than those when I met the Corales family who hosted me for three months in Costa Rica. I lived in Monteverde, a really small, touristy town situated within the cloud forest reserves. They were a family of five with three children—an older daughter, Tania, a younger daughter, Nicole, and Daniel, the middle son. In the entire family, only one person spoke fluent English—Tania: she was nine and I was fifteen. Needless to say, Tania and I grew very close. I thought I would catch a break with the whole language barrier when the teacher who picked us up from the airport spoke English. However, it became very apparent at the dinner that first night that even though my host mother understood me perfectly when I spoke English, she would only respond when I tried in Spanish. Even though we were supposed to only speak Spanish at home, Tania and I quickly

In Costa Rica with my host siblings.

came to an agreement as we waited for the bus on the first day of school. She needed to practice her English and after three days of trying to figure out Spanish, I needed a break.

Fifteen year olds should be full of fun and life, they should be having amazing social experiences but that wasn't the case for me in Costa Rica. When I went to Costa Rica, I expected so much from the experience that I was let down. I had no idea what the country looked like, no inkling of the culture, but I expected to have something in common with other kids I met there. That expectation was based solely on a misguided notion of the other. I was the other at Proctor because I was a Liberian girl living in New Hampshire. I thought the problem was my cultural background in the United States of America, so I enjoyed every moment I got to spend with my host family. My host mother Lideth is still one of the bravest and strongest women I have had the pleasure of knowing. She and her husband Heiner worked tirelessly to provide their children with a good education that would prepare them for the world. I was received with open arms into their fold. I am grateful and blessed to have had that family.

I was completely comfortable with my host family, but outside of that nurturing environment, I fell back into my silence. I spoke up when I was spoken to, but that was usually only in one-on-one situations. I spent a decent amount of my time and money at a sparsely populated coffee shop on the outskirts of town. Besides the coffee shop being unpopulated, it had good coffee and free wifi. All it took for me to find another place to escape my reality through my computer. I was living in Monteverde, walking the paths and streets of Monteverde, interacting with people in Monteverde, but I found myself ducking off the school bus a mile before my intended stop to sit in an alcove at a coffee shop until the setting of the sun dragged me away from my screen and into a cab. I always made it home in time for coffee and the chaos of having three kids under the age of nine trying to do homework and watch TV. I fit into that scene superbly.

Linda was at Proctor's campus struggling with social isolation from our peers, and I was in Costa Rica equally isolated from my peers. I accepted my situation so I didn't think Linda would do any different until I got this message:

9/25 3:33pm
Linda: I have some news for you
Pudu: Good or bad
Linda: I left Proctor today to attend my hometown school. I want you to know that I will visit a lot and you are welcome home any time and I wanna see you all the time bc I'm gonna miss you so much !!! You're my pudu and I love you and we will see each other a lot!!!!
Pudu: Why?
Linda: I just feel for me right now being home is best. Nothing's wrong with the school, it was hard to leave but for me this is best. But know that you are a part of my family now so we will be dragging you back here all the time and visiting u!!! I don't know what I am gonna do without u! I will miss hounding u hah
Pudu: Lin now I just do not want to back to Proctor. Did something happen?
Linda: Aw Pudu I'm sorry. No, nothing happened! You will have a great year I know it!! We will see each other all the time and (our other friend) will be there. Trust me you will have a good time:)
Pudu: I don't care I just I can't deal with Proctor you don't know how hard it is for me now I don't even have u but I'll be supportive and I'm happy if u r happy
Linda: Aw Pudu I'm sorry to do this to you. You will have a great year! Just don't think about it yet. Enjoy Costa Rica. We will see each other a lot and you will get to know everybody and make friends ! I love you and stay positive, you'll have a good time.

I took Linda's advice to heart, dealing with the situation in Costa Rica. I understood completely. I knew how hard it was being in a place where everyone said hi to you, yet no one stayed long enough for a conversation. Despite all my understanding, after I was done being brave, strong, and put together, I climbed into my bed, put my headphones on, and cried myself to sleep listening to "Little Things" by One Direction. It was Linda's band, and Linda's song, and I was so sad. I felt like I had lost another friend. It seemed I was the unluckiest person in the whole world, I gained friends just in time for situations to snatch them away from me. After that night, I woke up and went about my life as best I could. I told myself I was in Costa Rica and my goal was to not be concerned with what went on at Proctor. I still texted Linda and talked to her, but I didn't think about her not physically being at Proctor.

Four months of living in Costa Rica required a lot of adaptations in the way I thought and the things I decided to keep in my life. When I got to Costa Rica, being the picky eater that I am, I refused to eat any of the tomatoes in my food. I spent several weeks disassembling and reassembling my lunches and picking apart my dinners, before realizing that I couldn't beat them so I embraced the red vegetable-fruit. I also gave up on my stance against coffee. I will advocate for Costa Rican coffee any day. The stuff was so good I went from drinking hot chocolate with lots of milk once a day to drinking straight black coffee five times a day. The changes I had to accept in Costa Rica prepared me for the larger adjustments I would have to make as I returned to Proctor. I had become a part of a family and embraced their traditions and quirks, but I had to leave to prepare for my winter term at Proctor. A winter term without Linda. I couldn't help but feel like the floor was being pulled from underneath me.

The Foreign Exchange Student That Never Was

Linda

The transfer happened quickly. After the Birthday Eve phone call with my parents, I arranged a visit to Marblehead High School. I told my friend at Proctor I was going to a doctor's appointment and went home for the weekend. I remember that day very vividly. I don't remember feeling a lot of pressure to like the high school, but I know I wanted to. My parents were very good about reminding me that if this wasn't the right fit either, there were other options. I had been accepted to other private schools for high school, we could go back to them. We could figure things out.

On a Monday morning, I arrived to the high school with my mother and met the man who would be my first guidance counselor at Marblehead. He was a tall and friendly man who took a great deal of consideration in my revisit day and entry into the high school. I shadowed a student who was apart

Before my first visit to Marblehead High School.

of a cappella groups and chorus, interacted with her friends, and had a pretty good day. Everyone was trying to figure out where I was coming from and why I would ever walk away from boarding school, which was their wildest dream. A week later I was officially enrolled as a student, with an ID number and everything.

To this day, people are still trying to grasp where I came from. A couple weeks into Marblehead High, I was sitting in the school theater waiting for my a cappella rehearsal to begin when a student came up to me.

"Are you the new exchange student?" She happily asked.

"Uh, no." I said.

"Oh." Her smiled faded. Then she awkwardly walked away and I've been left to this day trying to figure out where the heck she thought I was coming from. Do I look that foreign? For a long time people asked me, "Where do you live?" or "Where did you come from?" I never knew what to say, because Marblehead is a public school so in most cases, I had to live in Marblehead. I usually said something along the lines of, "I live on the Neck but I've never gone to school in town before." Usually, people didn't have much of a response afterwards. Even my friends at Marblehead ask me occasionally about my schooling history and past trying to grasp the notion of my life.

"I've never lived anywhere longer than six years," I told them in April at a surprise party for two twins, who have lived in the same home their whole lives. Later that evening we flipped through their elementary school yearbook. It was crazy to see how many of my classmates they had grown up with. The longest amount of time I have ever gone to school with the same group of people was five years. I'm glad I've had a lot of movement in my life. Sure, it would have been nice to have started at Marblehead High freshmen year, but that would have excluded a lot of happiness in my life. For starters, this book would never have been written because I would never have met Pudu. There have been many incredible things that have happened to me and people I have met because I've placed myself in different environments.

With Kelsey White and Sarah Somes, two of my best friends, during one of my first weekends after the transfer. Seeing them gave me the peace of mind that things would be okay. No matter what, I always have them to cheer me up.

On October 30, 2013, I published an article on my blog called, "Lights. Camera. Action." It read:

"Everyday, a new script is being filmed ... Or at least that's how it feels for me at Marblehead High School. This truly is high school. The busy hallways. Crazy lunch blocks. The large number of students. It's as if I've been placed in a movie. Strange, really. Never in my life have I experienced such scenes...except on the screen. It's a journey I'm willing to take, but I often stop and think, where have I seen this before?

For those of you who ask, yes, I'm doing alright. It's been a crazy ride to get here, and I have a long way to go, but that's alright. Time can heal anything. I'm willing to wait."

This feeling hasn't gone away. The thing I always knew about Proctor was it didn't feel like high school, which isn't necessarily a bad thing.

There's probably countless people who wish they didn't experience high school, but for me, I wanted to know high school. And, sure, I complain about things like every other teenager, but that's exactly what I wanted. It's the crowded hallways, the one building for every class. It's what most of the world lives, I'm glad I know how it feels.

Proctor was all or nothing. It was dorm, class, field, dorm. An occasional trip to Pizza Chef was the farthest you could "get off campus," which says little. But I guess I honestly didn't need much else freshman year. I should have, but like I said, I wasn't unhappy. I just *was*. And Pudu and I weren't always stuck up in our rooms. We paint a secluded picture of ourselves, it's the same one in our families minds, but this wasn't our state all the time. We had each other—and while that may not have been everything we needed, it was enough for the time being. We played lacrosse together, watched ridiculous fail videos, spent money on cheap toys we never touched a day later. We were instant partners in crime, sisters so naturally to the core we could sit there and live with a little bit of tension and still know that we'd go to dinner together, regardless of one or the other's laziness to take out the trash. There's a unique form of magic mixed up in the strength of that bond.

I'm not sure I ever told Pudu this, but I wrote a play inspired by our friendship once. It didn't win the contest it was meant for, but nonetheless, it's a story I will always love. It followed the freshman year friendship of Jasmine and Darby. Through the course of the year, the two learn to rely on one another, especially when Darby's mother is sent back to war, where she subsequently dies in combat. Towards the end of the one act play, the roommates share this conversation at the funeral of Darby's mother.

JASMINE

Hey, look I know that today sucks and that every day for a while now is going to suck, and even the days after when you think you've moved on. Life is just going to suck. But, your mom was the kind of person that never wanted too much attention drawn to her. You owe it to her to continue that. She'd rather a legacy in a beautiful life of yours than a wasted one, you know that more than I do.

DARBY

Thank you.

JASMINE

For what?

DARBY

I don't know...For being that person I never thought I needed so much.

JASMINE

We're family now. That's what we do.

Pudu in *The Fiddler on the Roof.*

CHAPTER SIX

Ragged Mountain

Pudu

The emotions and insecurities I had suppressed in Costa Rica resurfaced once back at Proctor without Linda, along with the knowledge that my silence would follow me back to Proctor without Linda's presence to draw me out.

I remember having multiple conversations with the adults in my life about returning to school without Linda. I know they knew how hard it would be for me to adjust; they tried in their own way to assure me of their presence in my life. I had become so used to being alone and convinced of my ability to drive friends away, I continued doing exactly what I had done in Costa Rica to isolate myself from my peers.

I followed my routine, a routine that kept me sane until the end of high school.

Wake up, get dressed, eat food or not, go to school, go to sports, after sports read, have dinner, read, talk to family and friends, read, read until you fall asleep.

I was a bookworm before my freshman year, but by the end of my trip to Costa Rica, I was an obsessive bookworm who struggled if my routine was broken.

My routine quickly became one that didn't fulfill me at all once I got back to Proctor.

I spent most of my days outside on the slopes of Proctor's ski slope, Ragged Mountain, skiing. I skied for an average of 15 hours a week. During our runs, I loved how terrified I felt at the top of the mountain looking down towards the lodge—it added a spark to my routine. The spark was quickly dulled by my second concussion; I hit myself in the head with a metal water bottle when I slipped on a patch of black ice and landed on the ground. That simple fall caused me two weeks away from my sport, which meant I spent that time unwillingly alone in my room.

I felt lost without my new spark and I began searching for different ways to get it back unbeknownst to myself. I had no idea where to look until the voice of reason, Mr. David Pilla, my Wildlife Science teacher, paused in front of a frantic class filled with questioning students and delivered one of the greatest life lessons I have had to date. A lesson about fear and my life. He said, "You guys are so afraid of making mistakes, you won't even try."

I like to think of myself as an adventurous person. I know what fear is. I know what it feels like to launch my shaky limbs off a small cliff on a black diamond trail through the woods. I know what it feels like to get booed off a catwalk. I know what it feels like to leave your home and family behind for a new place. I had encountered fear and I had conquered it, or so I thought.

Dave's words came at the best possible time and opened my eyes to an injustice that I had subjected myself to—I was not living my life. I was participating in activities that were physically challenging and adrenaline pumping to make up for the fact that my life was as quiet as it was because I was afraid to release myself into the hands of the world.

With that lesson fresh on my mind, when the sheet rolled around to sign up for Spring Project periods, I picked the one that intimidated me the most. A four day trip in New York City, learning to sing, dance and act. I was among a group of nine girls with two teachers. We travelled around NYC in a large van from one workshop to another. I had my first dance classes on that trip. I stood on a stage for the first time acting on that trip. I stood up in front of a large group of people and sang solo for the first time on that trip. I still got the adrenaline pumping feeling, but the best part was afterwards when I could look around the room at all the other girls who had done it with me and smile. It felt great to know that I was accepted and appreciated and, in my insecurities, I would be uplifted by my companions.

Who were the Slaves?

As a young Black woman,
I often wonder, why I am a young black woman?
I often wonder where the black came to be among my young.
I have come to question the essence and the importance of
that blackness,
The reason for that blackness.
Why? Because when I hear the word black I think wrong, evil
and all that comes with the word dark.
Yes Black is beautiful, there is no doubt about that,
Black is beautiful.
The color is beautiful, the connotation is not.
Black is important it makes everything else better.
The color does that, the black young man is seen as a criminal
He is held down in the streets of Atlanta.
The black young woman is seen as angry.
She cannot speak her mind without fear of being called typical
The black young artist with the colored hair and a sweet slang,
Let me look at her and the word ratchet comes to mind.
Her freedom of expression is chained to the walls of society.
Blackness should be only color.

The Black in my blackness holds me down,
The black in my culture makes me inferior.
The blackness of my skin is not a mark against my strong
cultural heritage,
It is a representation of my strong, beautiful, colorful culture.
Take off the Black in the blackness, see the beauty in the color.
My black is beautiful, my black was a teacher, a preacher, a
leader, a healer, a counselor, a friend, a mother, a daughter,
a king, a son, my black was a civilization before it became a
slave.
Who were the slave? My blackness. Where did the human-
ness in us find its home? My blackness.

I am a young black woman.
Don't be confused as to what that blackness is.
That blackness is pride and it's beautiful.
It's Africa.

That Spring Project trip was the beginning of me stepping into the world and recognizing my place in it—on stage I got to be anything, in a song I could portray any emotion, in dance my body was free to to do both, but best of all, I was never alone in any art form.

When we got back to Proctor after that trip, I had had such a fantastic time with all the girls in the project that I had to figure out a way to preserve that feeling. That led me to drift away from my routine one Monday night. Instead of going back to my dorm after sports, I walked into the theater and auditioned for a part in the musical. I didn't get one part, I ended up with three. I became responsible for bringing three characters to life. I got to witness magic in the making. It wasn't always pretty; it wasn't always flawless. I learned pretty quickly that watching a show is the easiest part of the show. Joan Saunders, Terry Steocker, and their student crew taught me quickly that costumes weren't just bought, they were crafted. On the technical side of things, sets and set pieces were built from scrap early, then they were broken and built again. I saw the effort, the patience, the caring, and the absolute open mindedness, easy going nature that made Michael Littman an incredible director. I was with people every evening in that theater, exploring through the curtains, learning and creating. There didn't seem to be rules and signs, yet I still felt the rush.

I wasn't standing at the top of a mountain. I was under the lights in a warm theater, in the spring of my sophomore year and I found the musical "Little Shop of Horrors."

Pudu in *Urine Town* as Officer Barrel.

It's All The Same With Change

Linda

While nothing monumental changed senior year, every-thing changed.

Right now, many of you may be questioning, *What happened to Junior year?*

Nothing. In fact, Junior year was quite a good year for me. I gained an appreciation for my life and high school. I made friends, felt noticed in the community. But, nothing much happened, unlike Senior year, where information was spoken a mile a minute and life seemed like it was constantly moving.

I've never been so confused. I've never been on such a roller coaster of emotions than during the fall of senior year. The more I felt I knew, the more questions arose.

I made my vision for what I wanted in college very clear in the spring of Junior year. I had no intention of being in the middle of nowhere. I was not going to spend another four years repeating high school. I knew my passions; I wanted to get focused. And pretty early on the perfect school seemed to land in my lap. Emerson College. Located on the Boston Common, this city school offered the exact—breathtakingly amazing—curriculum I wanted. Students were passionate, hard working, and creative. Everyone had goals. Everyone was dreaming big. Emerson, it was the place. And while I didn't get the "this is it" feeling the first time I visited, as I did for Proctor Academy, I did have this feeling multiple times along the process. But, of course, we surveyed our options. I visited schools all over the east coast and even three in California. I had a film school category and a liberal arts school category.

As I visited schools and my interests grew, I had to fight the opinions of many. Liberal arts was the "better" choice to most of my friends and relatives. I knew I didn't just want a liberal arts education, which I would receive at the University of Mary Washington, a Virginia public school. I've been getting a liberal arts education for the last eighteen years of my life. And the last five years I've known I wanted to pursue creative writing. I didn't want to waste time checking off boxes just to graduate again. I wanted to get right to work. I was ready.

We visited around fifteen schools. I applied to twelve or thirteen.

I didn't have a real interest in most of the schools. A few were kept on the list in case Jack and I wanted to attend the same college. My mother's alma matter was there too, though it never felt right to me. I applied to half of the schools early action and the rest regular decision. The University of Mary Washington was the first school I heard back from. A large envelope with the words "You're in!" printed on the front shocked me as I arrived home from school. Mary Washington was the top liberal arts college on my list. While it didn't offer me the creative courses I desired, the tradition and culture of the school was warm, fun, and similar to much of what I had expressed wanting for the next four years. Being accepted to this school made the rest of the process seem safe, that anything could happen because I had a great school to go to, but that didn't stop my nerves a few weeks later as my computer screen loaded Emerson's early action decision. Getting into Emerson was largely about validation. It was the fact that a committee of successful working artists agreed that my stories held potential. It was the idea that they thought I could do it, be a writer, perhaps even make it in the industry.

Both acceptances made me excited, but I didn't allow myself to come to any conclusions until I heard from every school. By that time, it was clear. Emerson and Mary Washington were the two worth debating. For many months, I had lived with my options, with two very different roads to travel. Each offered something I wanted and things I wasn't thrilled about. I'd be happy at either school. When it came time to make my decision, I had visited Emerson and Mary Washington three or four times each. I'd seen them on good days and bad. I'd seen them on weekends and weekdays. I'd been to sample classes, hung around the surrounding area. I knew everything I could know about them. The decision just kept getting harder.

I think I was shielding my heart during this process. Because I knew halfway through my first tour of Proctor Academy that it was the high school for me—I knew. But then everything changed in a year's time, as I drove away from Proctor forever. So, I think I was trying to prevent myself from going down the wrong path, even though I knew from experience that a change of heart, or other kinds of change, was always possible. And that nothing was wrong with change either.

For two weeks, I tried not to think about the impending decision. But as any high school Senior will tell you, that's one of the most difficult things to do. The questions are always there, lingering at the forefront of your mind. Just as I'd begin to feel comfortable with one school, the panic attacks would begin. Not throat-clenching, can't-breathe panic attacks, but the fear that I wasn't making the right choice, that I really had no clue what to do, that I was missing something.

It was April 6th when I decided to write. I didn't expect to decide my future as I wrote my thoughts, but that's exactly what happened. Since I had kept my poker face on for so long around my family, writing showed me what I was really thinking. As I rambled on about what I liked about the two schools and the things I really wanted in my life, it seemed so obvious. Mary Washington felt very much like camp, with its many traditions. Its location seemed like the best of both worlds—small town, but close to a city. The people seemed real, and I liked that there would be a variety of interests represented on campus opposed to merely those hoping to make it big in Hollywood.

The question that really helped me solve my issues came from *Gilmore Girls*, a popular television show in the 90's, with a revival by Netflix premiering late 2016. Spunky single-mother Lorelai Gilmore is asked at one point, "What do you want? What are you willing to give up for that? What are you not willing to give up?" When it really came down to it, I knew the answer all along, I was just trying to fight it. Not because I didn't want to be happy or I didn't love the school—because I did—but because it was not how I envisioned my future. It felt like putting everything on hold, and I hated that.

I texted my camp friends Kelsey and Sarah the morning before I officially made my decision. Even though I knew they wouldn't fully understand, I had to try expressing some of my thoughts because I had gone two weeks without talking to anyone, trying to avoid more opinions haunting my own. That specific conversation didn't resolve anything, but I knew. I had come to know. So, I got up and was all ready to tell my parents, who were just leaving to go somewhere. I remember anxiously sitting around for a few hours, waiting, wanting to tell them...

When the time came, I couldn't even say the words without crying. I wasn't crying because I was sad, though it was hard to close the door that Emerson provided. It was the end of a tremendously long phase. It was emotional—exciting, terrifying, remorseful.

I know I've made the right decision. That doesn't mean I'm over Emerson, I'll never be. I honestly thought I was going there. I saw that for my life, and I wanted it so badly. I just have to trust that God inspired the words my thoughts drove me to write. I know I made the right decision. University of Mary Washington is the place for me. I'll go in with low expectations, allow what happens to happen, and make the best of it. I'm ready for this.

I empathized immensely during this decision process with Troy Bolton from *High School Musical 3: Senior Year*, who chose a school that combined both his passions, but what I really needed to do was answer that question from *Gilmore Girls*. I knew what I wanted; I knew what I wasn't willing to give up. This is where it has led me.

I believe we learn more outside of school than during class. Our lives are constantly changing, but in class we sit reading textbooks for an hour. It's a very static learning process, even including activities and videos. Whenever you are forced to learn something, the learning process is dampened. Life lessons come at us from any angle, even when we least expect them to. I think that's what makes them so impactful, we're not waiting for them to be understood, they just slip into our minds.

Senior year is filled with one giant life lesson, accepting the future, whatever it may be. And, I guess when I say the future, I really mean the unknown. None of us are really afraid of the future, we are afraid of what we don't know—whether it will be good, bad, shocking, magical or a combination of those emotions. Now into late April of my senior year, the idea of my college future has become as calm as it will ever be, but there are other factors in my life that are changing and which are teaching me this same lesson every day.

My house in Marblehead, with the basketball hoop I was playing at when I got the idea for my first novel.

My parents' realtor comes into the house in the evening with a chipper smile. She sits at the kitchen table with my parents as I head upstairs. It's happening, the six years are being engraved in official paperwork. My house is going on the market. For some strange reason, my family has never lived in a house longer than six years. We don't move on purpose, but for some reason the cycle of our homes has run like clockwork. Six years and it's time to move on.

It occurred to me the other day that not only would photographs have to be taken of the house, but of my room. I knew this, but I hadn't thought about it as my room, with my stuff. I remember when we visited our Swampscott house and the bedrooms were decorated. That was such a selling point for my brother and me. I got the room with the basketball jerseys hung on the wall and he got the one with the massive Hulk fist chair. And in 2010 when we visited this house, which belonged to an older gentleman, Jack again wanted the room that was to be mine. This time the decorations weren't what drew his attention, it was the view of the ocean, something that is so easy to take for granted. Knowing I won't always be waking up to this view allows me to appreciate it more. The little room with the classic two twin beds has become my home. It's weird to think somebody could be getting my icy blue room with the weird assortment of childish and teenage decorations. And I wonder what I'll be getting. Will it be a red-walled room with framed pictures hanging on the wall or a room with white lights and an office desk?

While I don't really care about moving—in the sense that a new environment is fine with me—it does feel strange knowing I'll never know the next house like I do my past homes. With camp and then college, I'll hardly have any time to discover the building's quirks this year. I don't know if I'll feel comfortable there, wherever it is, but I know I'll eventually learn to love my new home. I'm now realizing this is exactly what the rest of my life is going to be like. Because most of my friends will not be returning this year, camp will be different and college will be entirely new. Our world is constantly evolving, and so too must our lives to relieve our minds of boredom. Past memories, left behind but never forgotten, and new settings filled with unknown faces are the things that keep us alive and interested in our day-to-day journeys. I'm not worried about the negative parts of the future, because I know they are out there, inevitable, waiting for my arrival. As so many chapters of my life come to a close, I must stay focused on the positive—not out of anxiety or fear, but because that's what is worth supplying my energy to. I don't really think about it at this point. Every novel ends. So too must every life phase. So, I'll say goodbye to this house when the time comes and welcome the next house, along with all the new adventures my family will thus embark on.

Meeting Patrick Dempsey.

May 6, 2016

I just met McDreamy, the *Grey's Anatomy* star. I wasn't nervous when I saw him walk by me earlier in the night, or watching him speak on the panel. I was marveling at how normal it all felt, sitting near a famous actor, a member of

"Shondaland." "Shondaland" is the world made up of all Shonda Rhime's characters. A successful screenwriter of *Grey's Anatomy*, *Scandal*, and *How to Get Away with Murder*, she has made a home for herself Thursday nights on ABC. Patrick Dempsey plays the heartthrob doctor of *Grey's Anatomy* nicknamed McDreamy.

Dempsey was speaking on a panel, along with my mother's friend, at an event about youth philanthropy through sports. I listened intently to the conversation trying to find certain pieces to take away and use again in my own life, as I very much intend to be a part of a charity or foundation of some sort. But I spent most of my time watching Patrick, as I imagine most people in the room did. Noticing the way he half-sat, half-stood on his tall chair. Admiring how much attention he paid to every speaker throughout the entire night. He was fully committed and completely attentive to the discussion. He wasn't here because he had to be, because it was just another job. He believed in it and wanted to know more about the things the panelists had done and the wisdom they had to share. I listened to the way words flowed from his mouth and the gentle tone of his laugh.

And then I found myself thinking, one day I'll be at another event with him. That my dreams will materialize and our lives won't seem so polar opposite anymore. That I'll be a writer for "Shondaland" or have my own version of it. Maybe he'll speak the words I write. Maybe one day he'll watch or read something my passion creates.

And do you know what my second thought was? I'll never be in the same room with him again. And, maybe that's true, but I hate that I thought it. I hate that I let the normal opinions of everyone else became mine, even for just a blink of a moment.

I'm reading Shonda Rhimes' book *Year of Yes* right now. I think she's an incredible writer. She's honest and funny and transparent. But one opinion she expressed in her commencement speech at Dartmouth College, Class of 2014, keeps bugging me. "Ditch the dream and be a doer, not a dreamer," she encouraged the graduates, and she made some excellent points: "Dreams are lovely. But they are just dreams. Fleeting, ephemeral, pretty. But dreams do not come true just because you dream them. It's hard work that makes things happen. It's hard work that creates change."

And while I certainly don't have the credentials to do so, I disagree. Not with her conclusion— "Years later, I had dinner with Toni Morrison. All she wanted to talk about was *Grey's Anatomy*. That never would have happened if I hadn't stopped dreaming of becoming her and gotten busy becoming myself."—but with any suggestion that dreaming isn't a really powerful force in life.

I cannot fathom life as merely a doer. I am a dreamer. I dream every day and, honestly, I don't ever want to stop dreaming. These dreams, these fictional stories created within my mind, inspire me to pick up a pen and share something with the world. These unwritten stories churn the fire of my soul—they ignite my being, the very purpose of life here on Earth. I don't ever want to stop dreaming. Being a dreamer shouldn't be an undesirable character trait. It doesn't mean you don't put pen to paper and bleed words ritually. Dreaming accomplishes the same thing as long runs in the middle of stressful times do for some people. Dreaming is an escape. Dreaming is unedited thought. Dreaming is a late-night drive with the music blasting. That undefinable feeling you get after watching a movie that changes you. That nervous feeling in the bottom of your stomach. Dreaming is wrapped up in every aspect of life, it's the oxygen floating in the open air. Breathe it in and there's not a thing you couldn't do. Because if you can't dream, if you have no creativity and innovation, there's nothing to be done in the first place. You cannot be a doer without being a dreamer, but you'll never have more than dreams if you don't do.

That is what I believe. And while Rhimes may believe a

similar statement, her desire to bring down dreams is the opposite of mine. I say, dream. Dream and dream on, because we would not have the world we do had multiple people not first dreamt about new technology and then sought the resources to make their dreams a reality. Dreams and visions for a future aren't the problem, they aren't the thing stopping people. Fear and laziness and excuses stop dreams from formalizing themselves, but there'd be nothing to bring to reality if our minds were not given the freedom to think up whatever they desire. Change would be nonexistent without creativity. One of creativity's best forms of communication with us is through our dreams. Cut that off and there will be nothing for you to do.

So I sat at that high-rise table with a third thought: It will happen. I'll find myself in the proximity of Patrick Dempsey again. Maybe on a red carpet event or at a Network gala. Someday, somehow, I'll be able to stare him in the eyes and say, "I met you when I was 18. Look at us now."

And if you think that I am crazy, if you are reading this while shaking your head at my "innocence" and "naivety," maybe you have lost your capacity to dream. Or at least to think hopefully, with the optimism of youth. An eighteen-year-old should be thinking these thoughts. She should be dreaming about these "pointless" life encounters. Sometimes it's the smallest movement that changes the trajectory of a life. Sometimes all you need is one experience, one goal to pursue. You need something to look back on and say, "that was the moment." The moment I knew. The moment I set out for great success. The moment everything changed.

And sometimes it's better to understand that one moment will never be the only one you ever get to experience. Because the future is unknown, you might as well be hopeful and open to its possibilities.

Chapter Eight
Ocean Classroom

Pudu

I can't talk about senior year without talking briefly about junior year because a lot of things changed junior year.

I took to the stage after *Little Shop of Horrors*; I couldn't imagine my life without acting. I enrolled in a full year acting skills class and for a majority of the year I was the only student. I traded soccer for dance in the fall, and in the winter, I traded skiing for hockey and *To Kill a Mockingbird*, in the spring I stuck to lacrosse but I was running after practice to get to *The Fiddle on the Roof*. I found my place at Proctor and it led me to my peeps. Junior year I was still spending my free time outside my activities in my dorm, but it was a process and a journey, after all Rome wasn't built in a day. So, I'll skip the building and get to when it was built for me, that is senior year.

The saddest thing I learned my senior year is this: to some people high school is the peak, it is everything. It's the face of the mountain scaled and it's the summit on which to plant a flag. To me, high school is neither a peak nor a valley. It is simply a part of my life. I like to tell myself I'm racing anywhere, I don't have a destination in mind. I have learning in mind, so that's what I did my senior year. I studied, I learned, I made mistakes and I gave myself room to grow.

I started out senior year with Ocean Classroom, an off-campus program offered at Proctor through the World Ocean School. It was a brain child of Dave Pilla, and he's worked tirelessly to make sure it is still a part of the school. I was to spend nine weeks on a ninety-year-old gaff-rigged schooner sailing from Gloucester, MA to San Juan, Puerto Rico, down the east coast.

My memory of the weeks leading up to Ocean Classroom is littered with anxiety, but not for the obvious reasons— open oceans, swimming, watch schedule, people. No, I was dealing with the knowledge that I would be away for the nine weeks that my favorite TV show at the time would be airing. I had spent that summer educating myself in all the possible outcomes of the first half of the season of *Scandal*, and Roseway was leaving the docks on 24th of September, the day it finally aired. I begged Dave to give me some leeway to watch the premiere, but alas we were setting sail and the no technology rule was firmly in place by then.

The salon in Ocean Classroom.

Ocean Classroom was an adventure, a deeply educational adventure into nature and all its nuances. Roseway wasn't just a mode of getting from point A to point B; she was home and she was the most important tool on the adventure.

SHIP - SHIPMATE - SELF

That was the mantra, I had to learn pretty quickly that my way of operating for the previous three years would not fly or keep me sane for long. It wasn't self-shipmate-ship. If I didn't feel like interacting with the people on my watch and chose to wash and clean the galley all by myself within the space of an hour, I could do it but I wouldn't do Roseway justice. Thirty three people living in close quarters leave a significant impact. I worked the hardest I have ever worked in my entire life on the ship with the most nights of interrupted sleep. I quickly learned that only two things really matter to keep me healthy—eating and sleeping. Everything else would work itself out. Lack of food meant seasickness and seasickness meant misery no matter the time of day. Lack of sleep meant seasickness and lethargy—neither of those are useful in running a ship. My inability to function meant my watch mates couldn't adequately cater to the ship and its other occupants. That is never a good thing.

As we made our way down the east coast with the lessons quickly amassing on the appropriate ways to care for Roseway, the lessons on how to care for the planet followed. The grey areas taking care of the environment quickly became apparent with every large vessel that passed us. The changes in nature became apparent as our educators who had done trips like ours on the same route began to point out differences about above and below the water line. Whether it was coral reefs, or water samples that revealed a disproportionate amount of plastic waste, or our nets that were constantly going over the sides of Roseway to capture floating debris. The effects of life on land were plainly visible at sea.

We studied the chemical balances in ports and in open ocean, compared data, and did the math, but what stuck for me was this simple fact. The ocean was our biggest resource for nine weeks, but as soon as we got close to land we ceased to be able to use it. It wasn't good enough for making desali-nated water, it wasn't good enough to rinse our dishes, and it most definitely wasn't good enough to go for a swim, at least until we got down to the caribbeans. The adventures of Ocean Classroom left a lasting impression. I learned one thing for certain; the nature of things are uncertain in this world. Everything is uncertain, even change.

I got on a boat the fall of my senior year having not completed a single part of the college process. I was terrified, it's hard to recall any other emotions at this point, but I wrote a lot on Ocean to capture the moments and my first entry and last entry into my journal tell it best.

Ocean Classroom Journal

09/21/15

Lethargy

Many things about this voyage has me skeptical and it feels like rehab, away from mandated. A rehab clinic I signed up for not because I wanted to because I felt I needed it, but more like I did it to prove to the people who said I couldn't that I can. Not because I need to but just because I can. I have no idea what this is. I have no idea if I can make it to the end in one cohesive piece—in mind, body, and spirit. I guess that's the beauty and joy, but it's scary to not be able to fit in and the insecurity about a lot of things, trying to explain myself before I am questioned. I'm not gonna lie it's scary, terrifying and I feel awful but I can't break the habit. I don't know how to stand tall for what I believe and feel in a way that's honest to me and my story.

The instinct of silence for me now, I don't know if it's a safety mechanism or just what I want. Silence. Silence makes me think and feel and declutter and reassemble myself, like now. It draws me inward to my mind and eyes and focuses everything on that. I like silence but in the noise, it's a different dialect. I can't comment and be genuine because I am not of the space, I don't share memories, games, or dreams in common with any of these people. I have to think about myself; I have to conspire to change and it's not fun. I feel like I represent something which I want no part in. I want no part in being a cultural statistic, or even a sign of something different. I just want to be me and maybe I wouldn't be feeling this way if I just didn't shave my legs…

Two weeks after I cut my hair, on Friday, at 2:19am

Look onwards and upwards

It's starting to dawn on me that this trip is coming to an end. I'm excited to be going home to my family and friends but I'm pulling it in because I don't want to lose the importance of this day. There are a lot of things in between now and then and even more things between today and tomorrow but this trip has been valuable to me for many reasons. I learned how to calm down and be patient. I'm a collector of quotes and for a long time I would say to myself, "Patience is a virtue." I never really understood what that meant until I got on Roseway and was put into a watch group of the most easily distracted people. I've gone from telling people what to do 15 times in one minute to asking people to do things twice in ten minutes if they don't do it. I've also come to appreciate just doing it myself. There are a lot of things to be unhappy about on a boat, but there are also a lot of things that can make you feel really good about yourself; however, it'll never work without putting yourself, and others, in an important place.

Tales of The Roseway
I've known of a person,
for months on end.
A he or she, it mattered not.
The stories they told were
to me of beauty and struggle.
Simply put, the survival of time.
I waited and waited each passing day,
to meet this person
infused with such full a history.
I reminded myself of tales of each voyage,
that soon I will know, first hand of this homage.
For old men and young men alike
told tales of change I would find, within myself and the
world, for this person was simply that great.

The day arrived finally, I thought,

with apprehension and excitement,
for there was this person
standing proud, in her liquid bedframe,
But wait, stop, wait a minute.
This just can't be, she's
much smaller than in my dreams
and look at her name
held high above her mast.
This can't be Roseway.
Her pennant is shredded.
It only says Rosewa.

So there I was upon meeting this
great one, filled to the brim
with indifference and fear.
If I misjudged her look
I misjudged her fame.

Surrounded by noise and excitement,
as family and friends were anxiously
reunited, yet soon to be departed.
I fought my tears and sat
upon Miss Roseway.
"Well if you won't do it for
me this must be a waste
of my time."
With face faced forward
and bowsprit, high
she held me up indifferent

To my indifference.

Soon, oh very soon, families
amassed alongside the dock,
take ones and twos were
shouted and lines hauled away,
the Lessons suddenly began on how
To treat Miss Roseway.

Ugh I have to be awake for an hour
tonight, checking bilges
what the heck, they look the
same.
My God, how can a person
sleep with all this creaking?
Miss Roseway can't you sit still.
If you move at all at least
move faster.
With bowsprit pointed forward
decks slanted with
wind filled sails, and
incessant groaning planks.
Focused was her frame in this life changing
Voyage.

The days and weeks moved by
slowly at first,
then quickly disappearing.
Along with time,

came the views of
Hurricane Joaquin.
Whoever named it must have
been in a stupefied dream.

Scared? Yes.
Of this faraway thing?
Of course.
It had names of ships that sunk in the seas.
It made Miss Roseway
turn tail and hide.

Anchored in a Bay
with pelting winds and rain,
Here I came to know the true meaning
of wet misery.
Complain I did, in my mind.
"Miss Roseway, Miss Roseway
why must we stay here?
I've nearly met my stomach
with every cooked meal."
With bowsprit faced forward,
anchor chain fastened
Miss Roseway refused to be blamed.
Impatient as I am, I did not simply rest
"Miss Roseway, Miss Roseway
Miss Roseway, the decks are always
Wet, my fingers are pruned to the bone
And goddamn it we can't all fit in this

Salon."
Ugh oh ugh my brain is spinning.
It's starting to hurt with all this
Complaining.
I need a moment
just one hour to look in my
mind and find the answers.
(SEPTEMBER 2015)

The Roseway anchored near Vieques, Puerto.

Chapter Nine

Feel Your Pain

Linda
May 24, 2016
12:04 AM

I think it's important to remember that no matter our struggle, there are other people with greater problems. And beyond that, we're all struggling. So while you may feel alone and isolated in your pain, know that most people around you are suffering from the same illusion. Life would not know happiness without suffering, I believe that. And I think it takes time to heal. It's like a scar. At the day of the wound, the pounding of the pain is the only thing you can focus on. As the scab forms, slowly the pain numbs, until one day you look down at the mark and realize you'd forgotten it existed. And that, my friend, is when you have reborn—perhaps not entirely, nor as new as you'd hoped, but your world has begun to fix itself in the silence of your daily life.

Noticing is the first step to moving forward.

But I still think it's important to remember others. I'm not saying your pain isn't as meaningful or worthwhile as others' because it is. All pain is. Because if you don't take a moment to acknowledge your bleeding wound, it won't ever stop. In fact, depending on the damage, it could change your life. So feel your pain. Be in the moment with it. Cry. Scream. Blast your music. Dance. Do whatever the voice of your dark soul desires because that is how you will begin to heal. Just keep in mind, we all have different tolerances. We all walk our own roads, regardless if they seem similar. Be respectful of pain, I guess that's what I'm saying. Don't flaunt your suffering or lack thereof in another's face. I know we all grieve differently, but trying to rise above your suffering by making others feel worse will only deepen the damage of your wound.

I realized tonight that yes, I have overcome a lot these last four years. But these issues, these challenges could look so different in someone else's eyes. I didn't deal with immediate family death. My limbs are all intact. I simply changed schools. No big deal, right? Well, maybe to you. To me? It wasn't an earthquake, but my life certainly did shake—gradually, for a long time. Until I realized, in moments like tonight, standing in a dark room with strangers feeling my heart pound in the most unique way as I sing along to lyrics that have streamed out of my headphones for weeks, that I am happy. I am okay. I have made it, more successfully that I thought. Those mornings in the bathrooms are behind me. I do not know what tomorrow brings, but I wake up more confident than the previous day. That didn't happen overnight. It wasn't even something I planned for. It came like a season. Washed over me in a moment so pure, so blissful that I'll never forget it. Because I am so fortunate to be living the life I've led. To have the choices I get to make and the roof above my head. Hear me when I say these are not just words I feel obligated to say because I live in a preppy town with a house on the Atlantic Ocean. No. I understand that is the case. I get how privileged I am, and I thank God every day for the life he has paved for me. But I say this because we forget. So often we take it for granted. My parents don't have to do what they do for me. My brother and I don't have to get along. My friends don't have to respond to my flutters of text messages in the way they do. I don't have to be happy. But I am. All these things are happening to me, and I am grateful. Because I know pain, I know suffering. At my own level, I have been there. I have wondered what it all meant, the decisions we make and the impact the world has on us, and I have begun to find myself. And more so, love myself.

People say as a teenager you are supposed to make

mistakes and a fool of yourself because you don't know who you are. I've known for a while. It's been hidden beneath my shell. And slowly, I feel the armor cracking. Sure, I still feel the need to look the way people expect an eighteen-year-old girl to look and dress a certain way, but I'm allowing this fear and anxiety of fitting in to fall to the background of my mind. I'm more confident in the things I'm doing. I'm less apt to put myself below others based on superficial things. Am I perfect at that? Do I never feel insecure? Of course not. That's the hardest part about life, learning to blend your opinions with others and finding the balance of the two that allows you to live life to the fullest. But I'm getting there and that is what matters. Because when I look back at my life, when I see the things I've done and the places I've been...right now, this is the perfect ending to a four years of new beginnings. Public school wasn't what I thought it would be like, neither was Proctor, but in each I made a home for myself. I broke down barriers. I made a name for myself. That is strength. That is determination. And so as I swayed in the audience tonight, I realized, my problems at the moment, they are so small in the grand scheme of life. And how fortunate I am to say such a thing. What a blessed life I've been given to feel so positive, so open about the future and my current world. I look down, I can hardly see a faint imprint of my wound. Who knew such freedom existed.

May 29, 2016
Time Remaining: Two Weeks
I'm a combination of tired and awake
I've never known to date.
There's a numbness in my bones
and a fire igniting within my soul.
Chapters are filling,
flying to the end of their pages.

It's ecstatic,
like a midnight moon.
But I can hear the wolves howling,
chasing me from the distance,
catching up so soon.

I'm not scared,
though I haven't decided if I'm ready.
There is a steadiness to the rhythm
of life I lead, but in two weeks
choirs will be singing.
I'll be making my final walk out.
Tassels turned to the left,
my past finished with limited regret.
And tears full of pride.
Maybe the wolves will never catch up,
They'll get lost in the fog, but they tried.
Tried to end whatever might be coming.
But they didn't realize,
it's the midnight moon that
makes me howl just the same.
So as we all run in our own directions,
feeling the weakness and strength
of our last pages,
it's without a doubt our life changes.

But like stars,
our fates will be out there waiting
and our past will burn brightly for
longer than we will ever know.

Though I believe we will begin to understand slightly
that our purposes are worth fighting for
and our howls,
so mighty they be,
shall ring in the silence of
eternity.

The confetti and colorful lights in this picture represent to me life and
imagination. To me, there's almost nothing more beautiful than a concert, regardless of how well I know the artist. I'm always inspired.
All my worries fall away and everything feels right.

CHAPTER TEN
The Place I Am, My People Have Seen

Pudu

The dream is to do better than all my ancestors, those who came before me; unknown faces who without them, I would not be. I make it sound really poetic, but all the waxing lyrics aside, I push myself to live a life worthy of the time I will be given to live it, because life changes quickly. I often find myself in awkward and intimidating situations—like Costa Rica and like applying to a college even further away from home than Proctor. I didn't become that way overnight and that's the most amazing thing about my life. I have been molded and shaped by the fantastic people in my life. The first of those being my family—they gave me my name by being present in all my memories growing up.

I have a rather large and obnoxious family, complete with sometimes unending drama, but a family nonetheless. I have been blessed with the title of big sister, little sister, Irish twin sister and daughter.

Growing up in Ghana when the title of big sister hadn't been added yet, every morning, my older sister Amber, my older brother Arthur and I would sit on the low fence of a police station. The police station's fence served as a pick up stop for the school bus, and in the thirty minutes we waited we had the most fantastic discussions. It ranged from our weekends at the pool, to school events and crushes, but the most altering discussions were always about the future. What we wanted to be when we grew up. Cars drove by and pedestrians walked and talked about their daily lives in the Ghanaian equivalent of suburbia, time passed. Yet we projected ourselves into our desired future. For my sister Amber it rarely changed, she wanted to be a doctor, for my brother Arthur

End of summer family trip in Conney Island, August 2015.

and I it changed a lot, every time we had the discussion. I wanted to be a lifeguard and dancer, anything that I picked up during the week.

For the longest time that change was everything. I could be anything. That was the theme of my dreams and visions about my future. It was always shifting, never concrete and I realized as I got older that wasn't the norm.

Others had picked professions and stuck to it or were serious in their consideration, they didn't just imagine something and say it. I decided I had to find a future path and stick to it, so I said fashion designer one day and stayed there. Except staying there meant my future plans and visions were stabilized, no longer fun to dream and think about. I had an answer but I had stopped dreaming. For probably four years between fourth grade and eight grade I stuck with it.

However as life often goes, things change, the social landscape opened, I lost and gained friends, and career day came around. Everyone was excited, but I wasn't.

How does a fashion designer dress? That was my crisis. I looked through my closet at the sundresses and shorts I owned and that was the moment I realized I couldn't be a fashion designer. I had no idea what went with what, or what was fashionable, or even who the brands were. I simply pulled a purple dress off the rack and wore it. The end? No. I got to school and during the first class our teacher wants to know what everyone wants to be. I'm fourth, he looks at me and by his expression I know he can't tell what I am. I'm wearing a purple dress, my hair is pulled back and I have on flats. When he asked, "What are you?" I remember looking over at my best friend as she laughed and said, "Ask her again, she doesn't even know."

I had to give an answer so I turned back to him and said, "A writer." I want to be a writer; all my goals and visions in life involve stories that I want to tell or show. I now know that all my dreams as a child were stories I told myself and being a writer is the only way I can live all those realities. It's been a long time since eight grade; I now tend to describe myself as a story teller. That distinction is very important for me.

A story teller is someone who shares what others have forgotten, can't see, have distorted or misinterpreted. The biggest draw for me, however, is the appreciation of others, the look into the lives and minds of people who you see every day. I have this desire to explore the lives of others, to experience their emotions and portray their beings. It's an intense desire but I am severely disabled in this endeavor, I am restricted in the way I use my voice.

When I started at Proctor most of my discussions with my mother involved using my voice and not allowing myself to be overlooked or taken advantage of. I was resentful of her continuous prodding. In my mind I wasn't her, I didn't have the courage like she did to stand and speak up. I wasn't a Nobel Laureate who travelled the globe advocating for women rights and putting an end to wars in various countries.

Until I got to Proctor I hadn't had to use my voice; I had an entire family of opinionated people who covered me in their opinions. I didn't have to speak so I wrote. I was a writer, in journals and margins and little pocket notebooks. I poured my stories and opinions there. I was proud of my writings but when my siblings found it they often laughed and jested so I wrote in codes that only I could decipher. I had my own code as a story teller, no one else could understand, so it became useless, or so I thought.

I have felt for the longest time that my life was handed to me, it wasn't earned and I'm not entitled to it. That I don't have the power to change things. I'm just now realizing that that is true for everyone but some people are just better at pretending.

Life happens and I'm okay, and when I'm not okay, that's okay too. I don't know how to get rid of that feeling of being controlled so I just live with it. I take that feeling with me most places and I've adapted it to suit my personality. Life happens for me, it works out for me, so college wasn't on my brain when I was sailing down the east coast the fall of senior year.

The fact that most of my classmates on the boat had already applied and completed their common app didn't faze me. A super smart woman in my life sat me down and told me that college wasn't something to worry about and I decided to believe her. It was so easily done because my entire high school experience had taught me that plans can fall to the ground at any moment.

I had imagined my freshman year at Proctor that Linda would be there with me through the four years. That didn't happen. Looking at another four years and planning and picking a place was intimidating so I made it simple.

I didn't want to be on the east coast anymore, or at least I wanted to be somewhere warm and I needed the school to have a theatre or film program. I didn't really care about anything else, so when I got off the Roseway, I had a list of schools I vaguely remember making the past May that suited my criteria. One day as I was scrolling through Tumblr I saw a tweet from USC about Tony Goldwyn giving a talk. I spent the entire day reading about his talk at different points so I started to research USC. I just remember reading that USC had the best film program in the country. That immediately hooked me, more research revealed that USC wasn't just saying it was the best, they had actual proof of being one of the best. What made the deal even sweeter was the fact the USC fit all my needs. It became easy after I sent my application to answer the question that often plagues most college applicants. The first choice. USC was my first choice because it honestly suited all my needs.

The decision on what schools to apply to was painless, but I was a lot like my peers when the dates for decisions rolled around. I did forget what the exact dates were but I knew the time was dawning. I, however, couldn't bring myself to approach it with the same nonchalance from the application process. It was becoming very real that I would be living somewhere unknown for the coming four years of my life. It's much harder to face the unknown when the choice is taken out of your hand, so I looked outside of myself when the anxiety became too much. I looked to God and prayed for things to work out for me, for my future, and for my family. That's what I do when things get tough. I pray, because my entire family is built and upheld by prayer. Prayer is a part of my identity and that's where the feeling I described before comes from. I am not just an eighteen-year-old girl who went to boarding school in New Hampshire. I am much more than that. I am blessed to be alive.

I come from a country that endured years of war and civil unrest. My parents and grandparents walked miles and travelled miles to escape the shells of bullets. My older siblings and I were carried for miles and protected by my family across borders to get us to a safe space. I can tell this story because men and women alike risked being ostracized and discriminated in a new country. My mother, her sisters and my grandmother dared to start over so we could have this life. While making these choices to do better and be greater they prayed every step of the way, so I pray because my family is proof that it works. I'm not worried about a lot of things because they work out for me because of God.

I got my decisions spaced out so when the rejections came they were cushioned by the acceptance and waitlists. I didn't know I had been accepted to USC at first. I found out that two of my friends who were more dedicated students than I ever was in high school had been rejected and I assumed the same went for me. I waited until I went back to my room without any chance of leaving again before opening up the email. I don't know if I called my mom or if she called me but I do know I listed the decisions to her and as I was listing them with pros and cons USC remained my first choice.

With family before graduation.

Chapter Eleven
Last Week of High School

Linda

I've been writing a story the last couple of days. One of the main characters is about to write a letter about himself and he begins, "I suddenly have no idea where to start." I suppose this is how I'm feeling now. I want to tell you everything. I want to capture the last week of high school in the perfect way, but that is just impossible. Words may never seem enough for this portion of the story, but I'm going to try anyway.

High school ended like a blink of an eye. Suddenly it was all happening. I felt emotions I had no idea I would feel.

I wanted more time.

I couldn't decide if I was ready. Even after four years of being ready.

For a long time, I was never sad about graduation and leaving Marblehead High. I was ready, and offended when somebody would mention, "you haven't had the full experience of high school if you're not sad." To me there was nothing wrong with being sad, but there also wasn't anything wrong with just being ready. A good or bad experience wasn't determined by the emotional impact leaving had on you, I believed. The night before graduation, it all hit me though. It was in my gut, the indescribable feeling of not enough time. The week prior came rushing back into my mind, having passed so quickly, and graduation day lay before me like a canvas ready to be painted, but I was afraid of what might be—with so much unknown beauty available for creating.

On the Monday of the last week of school, a chapter of my life ended. Being Editor of *Headlight*, the school newspaper, was a position I wasn't aware I really needed when I applied, but couldn't be more grateful for.

What I liked most about the newspaper was that it was for a purpose. The work I created—sometimes seamlessly within minutes, other times more forced as the clocked ticked on Sunday night—reached community members within the week. People I knew and will never meet all over this town pick up the *Marblehead Reporter* and flip to the *Headlight* page to hear from three or four students per week about anything—sports, music, events, editorials.

An athlete competes weekly, he gets praise and feedback regularly. Typically a writer writes, but she may not always have a reader. The newspaper provided that. This position of leadership gave me a voice, a larger role in my class. I felt validated in the work I was doing, and noticed in a sea of students.

The newspaper became more than just the ability to write. It opened my mind to be more thoughtful of all community happenings. Though I'd lived in Marblehead for many years at this point, I hadn't yet immersed myself in the town's traditions because I wasn't a steady member of the public school system. Traditions—whether it's just sitting as a family over a holiday meal or running around a field in an intense game of football—can change a life experience. Traditions take us out of ourselves; they open us up to the community and a world greater than our small personal lives. They help us leave a mark on the world. The more I grow and the older I become, this mark takes on greater meaning. The summer after senior year, I'm working as a camp counselor. Our theme for preseason is, "I was here." We listen to Beyonce's song a lot and talk about the impact our jobs have on the campers. It all reminds me of the people in my life who have made a difference—the friends, teachers, and even famous people I've never met.

As Editor, it was my turn to focus on the town, and what the people wanted and deserved to read. I recognized early on the privilege I had been given just to be Editor of a newspaper, regardless of its size. So many schools these days don't have the means to fund such an extracurricular. I was lucky.

As the "quiet girl" and the one people often don't seem to notice in a room, my gaining this visibility and trust was enlightening. It makes me confident that there are always people who see through facades. There are always people who look for the ones who may not be the loudest, most popular in the room, but who have just as much quality to share. I'm grateful that our faculty advisor and the editors who preceded me saw this during the application process. Although I was proud to list this position on college applications, I had joined the club for greater purposes. I joined to do the thing I love most and to be surrounded with like-minded people. I joined to continue history, share something new with Marblehead, and, fitting in with my goals during the start of my transition to MHS, to get involved with as many clubs as possible. *Headlight* became my very own headlight, helping me forge my way through Senior year feeling more confident in the person I'd become and proud of the craft I'd identified myself with for years. I found fellow students who understood the joy words produce and their purpose in the world.

But *Headlight* ended leaving me with an unexpected feeling. The feeling of time having run out before anything was really done. When I applied for the editor position, I filled out an application with all my ideas—a social media account, attempts to gain more writers—but once the fall began I fell into the old routine of past editors, waiting until things were settled until I implemented many of my own changes. Yet, things never settle, and because I waited, I missed my chance. That's not to say I didn't do anything. I certainly did, but there was so much more I could have done had I lived as if I hadn't received the position yet. Had I been more proactive, jumping on all the opportunities I could have.

Life goes by so fast.

We think that time is by our side, but time is nothing in reality. We must be on top of our life, actively pursuing what we want instead of waiting for the right moment to arise. I've been reminded of this. As I move on to greater things in life—college newspapers, real world jobs—I hope to achieve larger things in similar ways as I aim to achieve my daily goals, with pursuit always on my mind. I think because *Headlight* wasn't, to me at the time, the same thing as my dreams of being a creative writer, I didn't chase the opportunities like I could have. I saw the newspaper's limits, and I stayed within them instead of attempting to stretch the boundaries. And while there's nothing wrong with that, I've learned to strive for more out of myself, and everything I'm a part of, for that matter.

I ended my final *Headlight* article quoting actress Troian Bellisario, "embrace failure and fear as if they were your oldest and best friends and dance, don't walk, to this new beginning." I need to always remember that as I move forward in life. Eventually I want my job to be something that makes change in someone else's life, and I want it to be positive change. Whether or not you agree with me that TV and film have substantial impacts on us, I feel there are too many things in life that stay in our memory for negative reasons. Too many people we let linger in our lives for the wrong purposes. I want my words, my life, to be positive. It won't always be pretty and not everything I do will be meant for great purposes, but I hope when all the work is left on the table, it will be worth the struggles. I know some work has already paid off. I've lasted through what felt like never ending stress, and I've already reaped some reward.

Stretching boundaries is something I've grown accustomed to through high school. Going off to boarding school in a distant state at age fourteen snapped me out of my comfort zone, just as spending two days in Maine white water rafting with a majority of my graduating class did.

While some students waited all four years in anticipation

for this senior trip, I wasn't one of them. Coming onto my horizon late Junior year, I wasn't sure I would want to venture along. The physical weather conditions weren't as much of a factor as the people were. I needed to make sure I would walk away from that trip better than I was entering it. My life didn't need to change, but I wasn't going to pay to spend a weekend miserable. So, I waited. I patiently didn't make up my mind until very close to the deadline day, when I knew I had multiple friends accompanying me. And my life didn't change, but my happiness rose.

Twin Pines Camp.

Like most things in life, initial uncertainty quickly faded into free-spiritedness. After a seven-hour bus ride, in which our bus driver got lost, we arrived at Twin Pines Camp, which was much nicer than what I was expecting. My friends and I canoed around the lake, swung on the swing set like children, and talked—about TV shows, when dinner was, and anything, really. Conversation flowed like the waters that surrounded us. All the seniors gathered in the same grassy area, playing basketball, catch, volleyball, and frisbee. Some jumped into the cold waters and kayaked. And while people were certainly in their friend groups, it felt whole. We felt like a class. Sure, this was only one-third of our graduating class, but maybe that made it better. It got rid of the ones who'd bring nothing but negativity. It made it so no matter who we were with, whether we knew them well or were only just being introduced, we had a connection. We were embarking on this adventure together. We had made it.

The whole trip I could feel my shell falling away, cracking with every joke and word spoken. That is no light feeling. The ability to be around people as your true self is something I've only really felt at summer camp. And even that took time.

Time's been the biggest illusion and lesson of high school. It's nothing and it's everything. It's what carries us through the days. Has us counting down the moments that pass us by. Time is always by our side, or against us. We're racing with time, whether it's real or not.

And then it just goes. Washes away before we've even realized what's happened. And that is when we are left with the moments that survived time and the future that awaits with the next ticking clock. In moments like a graduation, all you do is wait and think of the passing time. Think of the goodbye.

I thought about it a lot. Felt it. Imagined.

A lot of this imagining happened late at night, occasionally as the sun began to rise miles away. When music was all my ears could hear and words were the only thing on my mind. Words of stories, of worlds and marvelous people I'll never meet. Words so beautiful, my mind wanders trying to determine the best way to bring them to life. Through this wandering, my thoughts often drifted to high school. To the end. Thinking, feeling, imagining. Preparing, maybe.

I found myself binge-watching childhood videos at

three in the morning one night. I landed upon *High School Musical 3: Senior Year* and was struck so emotionally by one of the simplest scenes in the movie—a movie I'm not afraid to say I've seen more than a handful of times. I never really noticed it before, though. One of the main characters, Troy, turns around to his father, smiles at his dad who does the same, and then hugs him before leaving for graduation. It's only an eight-second scene, but it's so real. I've been in that situation; I can feel it. In the gentle smirk of Mr. Bolton's smile. In Troy's pause before leaving the gym, realizing the pride and mixed emotions he and his parents feel about high school ending and college beginning. About things changing. It's one glance that says a million indescribable feelings in one, but most importantly, I think it says, "thank you." Thank you for helping me get through these last four years and allowing me to continue this journey for another four. Thank you for supporting me, challenging me, and, in your own way, thank you for letting me go. This scene reminded me how universal everything I have felt this year is; how my journey to graduation hasn't been exactly what I've watched in the movies or on TV, but it's been mine and now it ends, just as everyone's has on screen.

The night before campers arrived to camp last summer. It was the beginning of a new era at one of my favorite places in the world.

We each live different lives, but in moments like gradua-tion, we come together as people. We clap for our friends of ten years or two. We cheer for the ones we never talked to and the ones we looked forward to seeing every day. Somehow, all the years add up. The tears, the cluelessness, the hours study-ing, and the early morning meetings. It makes sense; it feels worth it.

I'm a big planner, I like to know what my days and weeks look like. For a while things were calm, but I knew the mo-ment graduation hit, everything would change. Camp was fast approaching. Then came college, a whole new everything. During that time, our house was being packed up and my parents were embarking on a new life in a Boston apartment. It was all coming, just days away.

I didn't tell most people about the move. Pudu was of the few who knew, and when she texted me one evening about how I was spending one of my last nights in my house, it slowly started to seem real. I never really get attached to a home like some people, probably because I've moved around a bit. But I do like this house. I think it's cozy and simple and beautiful. It's nothing special, except for the view, but that's why I like it. I like my room, and the basketball hoop, and even the gazebo I never spent enough time in. I think one of the weirdest parts about moving is knowing that the next family already has plans to tear down the kitchen, for instance, and renovate it. That if I ever were to come back here, it wouldn't look like my home.

This is also the home that birthed *Street Smart*, the first novel I've written. The Bridge family lives in this home, with the old-fashioned stove and the "cruise ship view." The main character Sam lives in my room, though it is decorated differently, and Nick lives in Jack's, and the grandparents live in the office. And David makes a life-changing decision at our kitchen table. Nick throws a chair out the window on the other end of that same table. Sam gets locked into her room with her mother Kelly for hours studying. Now, I know most of you don't know who any of these people are, but all you really need to know is they are more than fictional characters of my first full-length novel—they are my heart and soul. They are the characters and stories that have lived within me since seventh grade and led me to become the passionate storyteller I am today. And they started in this house; their lives were inspired by my life in this house. 339 Ocean is the Bridge family home, so it's sad to say goodbye to that.

But at the same time, I am very aware that the Bridge family will live on in the homes and hearts of the people that read *Street Smart*. I'm aware that as my surroundings change, so too will their's. And while their home may not be exactly what mine was, at least I'll always have a time capsule of 339 through them. That's something special most people never get.

Another thing most people don't feel is the confidence to be okay with few signatures in their yearbook.

At the end of our Senior Banquet, a five-hour event consisting of dinner, awards, and a hypnotist, I received my first Marblehead High School yearbook. Gathered in the cafeteria, everyone scrabbled to get as many names in their book as they could. Me? I made sure to get a handful of inscriptions from my friends, who each wrote meaningful notes, but I didn't care about numbers and names. I didn't need one hundred "have a great summer!" notes. I was very specific about not wanting to spend my high school years as somebody with loads of fake conversations and relationships, so I didn't need to memorialize it in ink that way.

"Do you have any regrets?" the Editor-in-Chief of the *Marblehead Reporter* asked me just after my graduation. I'd grown to know her through my internship at the *Reporter* for the five weeks prior to graduation during Senior Project.

"No." I shook my head with confidence, perhaps realizing the honesty of that statement for the first time myself. No regrets. How many people can say that? Of course there are things I wish I hadn't done, immature mistakes I made, but I don't really regret anything.

People put a lot of pressure on moments. I'm one of those people myself. We've been programmed to believe in order to have the experience of high school, we have to be a certain way, do certain things. These four years have shown me that you don't need to follow the trends, and you probably won't have *the* high school experience. Sure, bits and pieces may feel like a movie, but we need to forget about the pressure, which is much harder to do than say, I will admit. This idea of high school people have imprinted in our minds is false. Just get out there—whether your entering high school or any other part of you life—and live it. Don't stress too much. Let a moment be a moment, and move on once it's a part of your history.

Make the conscious choice to live for what you want rather than follow along a path you never had an interest in anyway. This decision will liberate you. I've felt it.

Walking into graduation (on the right).

Holding my baby cousin on Sunday morning, his hands wrapped around my fingers, it all came full circle. It feels like forever since I was that small, but eighteen years passed and I grew up to graduate. What will life be like when this little one graduates?

When the time came, we threw our caps in the air like tentative children given the opportunity to be reckless. Our leashes had officially been taken off, yet still in the comfort of our high school, rules seemed worth following somehow, even to the most reckless students of all. I saw nobody cry, nor any out-of-the-ordinary emotions. Just tentative smiles. Everything was over, just as we'd practiced a few days earlier, and nobody knew quite what to do or how to feel.

I've never been one who needs a lot of attention. Popularity isn't what I strive for. With that said, I wanted my family at my graduation. I wanted a crowd. I've spent a lot of high school searching for my people, carving a place for myself in a tight-knit community. At the end of it all, I wanted to walk away with my people, those who have always been there, and one friend who began the journey with me four years ago.

Despite the great trouble it must have taken, a plethora of family members and friends made it. I could hear them hollering from their seats in the gymnasium as I walked across the stage to retrieve my diploma. A diploma I worked hard for, that tests and official documents said I couldn't achieve from a public school. A diploma from a school I never had an interest in attending. A diploma that proved it's all possible.

I'm not just talking about graduating. To me, that was always possible. I never had a doubt in my mind that I would graduate, though I know that is a real worry for some people. The accomplishment for me was coming out better than I began.

High school took a quiet girl and allowed her to become self confident.

I left New Hampshire for more, and here I was accepting it. Graduation. It's no regrets. No looking back, wondering if things would have been better if I didn't transfer. Because I know. God delivered. That blink-of-an-eye rainbow I saw on the cement as I walked from my dorm room to the theater Sophomore year praying for a sign was everything I thought it was. It was a helping hand, ushering me to accept the decision. Rise up.

I rose, with trembling hands hidden in my pockets. I followed an invisible rainbow back to Marblehead, Massachusetts with nothing but faith.

And, then I stood, two feet on the floor, hands extended. No hiding, no uncertainty. Prayers no longer packed with hopes and wishes, but thanks and blessings. How did I do it? Was it all with just God at my side? Of course not. It was my family. My friends. It was Pudu, not letting one decision separate us forever. It was all the stars in the universe aligning in just the right way. So unknowingly beautiful that if you blinked you might have missed it.

I'm glad I kept my eyes wide open, because this journey... This is one story I never want to forget. It's a friendship I can only hope burns as long as the sun is bright and the stars are magic.

The day before my graduation, during a covershoot for *And It Begins*. You can almost feel the joy that comes from our friendship.

CHAPTER TWELVE

The Shaping of the Perfect Pudu

Pudu

Ideas come at the weirdest times. I like to think of myself as a professional procrastinator, some of my worst and best work is done in a frenzy of anxiety and tears. I was frantic as I sat behind my computer trying to think of a solution to my problem. I needed to come up with a plan to fulfill the requirements for Senior project in order to graduate. Senior Project at Proctor is a three-week period of time dedicated to completing an idea proposed by a member of the senior class. I would like to point out that there are limitations on those ideas, but as long as they are educational, enriching, and fulfill the requirements to graduate high school, they are green lit. I, however, had left writing my proposal to the last minute possible.

I had been envisioning my Senior Project since my sophomore year, yet the time came and I completely forgot until an assembly announcement jarred me. I had four days to write a proposal, find a mentor to monitor my progress, find a sponsor to be a liaison between me and the school, and I needed signatures from all the adults in my life for the project to be put up for consideration.

The global-scale project I had in my mind shrunk. I needed people on campus, and I needed a space on campus to work. I had taken up black-and-white photography in the winter again, so spent almost every day in the dark room. I found my space in Slocumb, I had a fantastic teacher I admired and I knew would be helpful. I found my person. I just needed a proposal.

Perfect Pudu is perfect according to perfect Pudu standards.

That's my mantra, I came up with it on Roseway. In essence it means the person I am is the person I am meant to be, so as I thought about Perfect Pudu a question came to mind. How did Perfect Pudu become perfect Pudu? That is a really easy question to answer.

People make Perfect Pudu.

For me, the smallest instances make the biggest change—a simple phrase, a simple question, a single moment. These are the moments that stand out the most to me, when I watch someone react to something in a way that is unique to them. My mind takes those instances and splices them together into a catalogue. That catalogue becomes the basis of reaction; it's a book of lessons for any situation I'm ever in.

My senior project, due to the circumstances, became a black-and-white photography book in which I aimed to celebrate and appreciate ten people at Proctor who had inspired me. I named it *The Shaping of the Perfect Pudu*. I would sit down and have conversations with the people I selected and tell them the ways they impacted my life. Beyond that I hoped that it would allow me to know more about these people, because most of them I had only known in passing.

I defeated the odds of time. I came up with a proposal written in a single night, I outlined my plans, all on the fly, and I had it printed out and ready for signatures.

This project wasn't difficult, it quickly developed a soul, an essence, that went perfectly with the plan. *The Shaping of the Perfect Pudu* was not a requirement I fulfilled in order to graduate, but rather a passion project in response to the moments in my life where one person completely unknowingly changed my outlook on the world.

I prefaced the project as the Proctor edition because Proctor has been a lot of things to me over the years. I somehow only realized how much it had truly changed me at the end of my journey.

The bravery I commonly applaud myself for is something that stems from my time at Proctor. I'm brave enough to experience new things. I'm willing to jump on the ice, dance on stage, or even sail the oceans. I loved and learned throughout all those experiences, but I wouldn't have been able to do any of it without Proctor. I'm not just talking about the opportunity the school provided for me, I'm talking about the people. I am who I am today because of a lot of people dedicated their time to influence my decisions.

Before I talk about people who are in *The Shaping of the Perfect Pudu*, I'll talk about one person who should have been there but isn't.

Jen Summers had been my acting coach, director, and overall motivator my entire Junior year. She was an actress, a writer, a teacher and, best of all, I trusted her with my work. I spent hours with Jen and her dog Lucy my Junior year, our conversations spanned multiple parts of my life and she got to know me incredibly well. I learned more about who I am because of Jen, I would stand on the stage and act out my scenes, reluctantly and over and over again Jen would turn the mirror towards me.

She would force me to look at myself and find the traits in myself that I liked, disliked, or didn't seem to know I carried. I had to deal with myself on stage.

It was a first for me, dealing with the actual Pudu. Not the programmed one with the routine that just went about her day. If something crappy was happening to me I had to deal with it, acknowledge it and let it go before stepping into a character. I couldn't just lock it in, because I had to leave myself to become the character of the day.

The invasiveness of the process was taxing, I would leave acting on Fridays and just sink into my bed either staring blankly into space or pumping myself up for practice. I did it though, every week I went back and loved it so much more because of how much work it required. I have a lot to thank Jen for, as my acting coach, she could have simply pointed me in the directions I needed to go, but instead she decided to walk the path with me.

A person can mean a lot to you and you'd never think to tell. Their life would mostly not change because you share, or don't share, but I like to think it's better to share, especially if it's with gratitude.

I tried to extend gratitude during senior project, whether it was simply by being around someone and having a conversation with them, or offering to help someone by joining in an activity because it allowed me to be present and remember my last moments. I still had obligations to some of my classes but for the most part I was creating my own schedule, I was doing the things I wanted to do and something amazing happened in that three-week period.

I realized what the reality of being older was, the responsibility for myself, my actions, my work, my social life—all of it was mine to mold as I pleased. I wasn't afraid though, as I talked to the individuals in my project I couldn't help but feel the community that was Proctor. It felt almost like their hands were blessing me as I walked away from each interview. I was prepared for the world by the people who surrounded me and I couldn't even name all of them in *The Shaping of*

Kelly Y. photographed for *The Shaping of Perfect Pudu.*

the Perfect Pudu. Here is an expert of what I created during Senior Project:

Indira
> Names that are hard to learn,
> Are names worth remembering.
> They can be a bothersome burden to the bearer,
> Their spellings often the source of frustration.
> Pronunciations a constant well of irritation.
>
> Your name is to be remembered,
> Through your acts, your voice!
> You've managed to accomplish,
> A feat! Simply a grand feat.
> A solid force of nature,
> So curious about earth's creatures.
>
> From eight years of life's breath,
> Your voice has risen above the noise,
> Sometimes a vessel for it.
> Your words are fully formed,
> From ones I formally misunderstood.
>
> Your questions are a challenge,
> Do better, think harder, have fun.
> In your name Indira McIntyre,
> There is now a strong-willed,
> Able-bodied girl, my crazy sister friend.

Betsy
I had a fairy godmother, at least I convinced myself I did. I had a fairy godmother who signed her notes, Betsy. Her notes turned up at random points, usually after I'd taken a

step outside of my routine. She reminded me of the importance of expressing myself in those little notes.

It turns out she wasn't really my fairy godmother, at least not in the Cinderella way.

I know who she is now, I know she didn't really know who I was. It's okay though, until last year I didn't know who she was, but it didn't stop her. It did not stop her from helping me grasp a message that I desperately needed to hear.

My insight, my story, my perspective, my voice, they're all important. They matter.

(Proverbs 31:10) Who can find a virtuous woman? For her price is far above rubies.

Dear Cope,
I never thought I'd find God in our friendship, I wasn't looking for him when you entered my life. I had forgotten what it felt like to see his presence reflected in the life of someone other than my family members. I am constantly in

Ani and Indira M. photographed for *The Shaping of Perfect Pudu.*

Sarah M., my friend and advisor, photographed for *The Shaping of Perfect Pudu.*

awe of your bravery and openness in expressing the joys of your religion; you manage this with the patient understanding that not everyone will appreciate it. I've witnessed you educate people on subjects ranging from history to quality TV. You fascinate and inspire me everyday with your willingness to share your excitement no matter the subject. I hope as you continue to grow into the virtuous woman I know you are becoming, that you never lose sight of how important your voice is at any table, no matter the subject.

P.S. I want my god baby, so don't forget.

Love, Lady Broch Tuarach Pudu.

My introduction to teachers at Proctor was Patty Pond, my Orientation leader. On our third day of hiking, she was supposed to give us a breakdown of Proctor's Green Book, but instead, she baked us a chocolate cake and told us to rip up the Green Book to make a bigger fire.

Looking back now, I see that as the first instruction to becoming the person I need to be.

I was in a situation that wasn't particularly fun, but what

I needed to do before I could come into my own was to rip up the pages that held me back and burn them.

Patty was followed by a slew of teachers, who weren't just my teachers, but also my coaches, my dorm parents, and my friends. Everywhere I looked in Proctor's community there were people rooting for me. They were challenging me to be bolder, braver, faster, tougher, and even smarter.

I used my time on Senior Project to pay homage to small moments like that; seemingly insignificant moments that pushed me into the universe. I spent forty-five hours working on the project. Hours in the darkroom developing prints, writing a blog and poems for the project, and formatting a photo book. It was a labor of love; a way to say goodbye to my community. Most of all, it became a way of reflecting on the times I'd had at Proctor. It was one final push into the heart of Proctor to create something tangible to give back.

I started my journey at Proctor with Linda and I believed we would travel the road of high school together. It didn't turn out that way. Of course, as a freshman, I was purely focused on our physical presence in each other's life at the time. Time and circumstance has a way of changing our plans for the future; that's just the way life is.

Singing a solo at graduation.

The Toast to Sisterhood

I drove almost seven hours in a car with my mom, my little sister and uncle to Marblehead. I wasn't stressed, I was dazed, I had a deadline to meet for this book and it was fast approaching, yet it was the last thing on my mind. I hadn't hit a wall per say, but I had taken a detour. I am writing a book about my time in high school, to me that concept is baffling. I'm watching the hours tick down on this drive, listening to Beyonce, Angelique Kidjo and Fuse ODG. I'm running stories and characters through my head and it hits me.

I'm going for Linda's graduation; except I'm not really going for Linda's graduation, I'm going to spend two nights at Linda's house before she walks on stage to receive her diploma. Those thoughts kept running through my mind.

I remember when I walked on stage to receive my diploma. It wasn't with feelings of pride and excitement over goals accomplished, but more so, anxiety over what I knew my mother, who was giving the commencement speech, had planned.

I refuse to taint that memory with nothing but joy. I'd walked onto the stage to receive my diploma. That was the goal, right? After four years? Wrong.

I hugged the chair of Proctor's Board, the Dean of Students, and then I got to my mom, she had already reached into her bra and pulled the wad of ones. The tossing of dollar bills on me began, followed promptly by the prods to climb on her back. Of course I did it, with great reluctance. I finally hugged the head of school, took my picture and exited the stage but as I began the walk back to my seat I heard my name being called. My guardian Abigail Disney, or Aunty Abby, was calling me. I looked to my seat where my friends were laughing and quickly ran towards her arms opened. I can still hear the sound of my sandals on the wood platform.

It was a memorable graduation, I've watched all my

elder siblings before me graduate, seen the spectacle that is made by my family. I looked forward to it happening to me for much of high school. It's a big deal to graduate from High School, especially if you consider Liberia, a small country where much of its population is undereducated. For me to graduate with my family cheering me on in the stands was wonderful, forget the fact that the diploma didn't really mean much to me, the hugs I received as I scrambled across that stage meant the world to me. I made my family proud, their work was not wasted.

Being embraced by my mother on stage.

I dozed in the car as we drove, wanting to eat and trying very hard to prop my little sister Nehcopee's head so she wouldn't startle in her sleep. It was a short journey to visit my friend who was about to celebrate a milestone I walked through two weeks before. We were writing a book about the longer journey of high school and I was anxious about what Linda would have to say about my progress.

Progress and journeys are words I've heard a lot in the weeks after my graduation and they are words I'm trying to work out of my vocabulary. It's terrifying. When I went to bed the night after graduation the one thing I had to ask myself was, *What the hell happened here today?*

I enjoyed the party and the presence of my friends and family. I enjoyed the attention. I most definitely enjoyed the presents, yet for some reason it didn't feel like a momentous moment in time; it felt like the passing of time.

When I sat at the table with Linda's family members, now my family members, surrounding us the night before her graduation, I fought the urge to lean over and say, "Don't expect an epiphany. You will have less ground beneath your feet after today." I fought it back.

I don't feel like the last four years of my life were an accomplishment. I don't think of the last four years of my life with a diploma in mind. I think of the last four years of my life as meetings. Multiple meetings in the same rooms, with different people, each individual bearing a message for me. Some of them were private, some incomprehensible for now, some loud and glaring, but most were touching, inspiring and moving.

This memoir isn't a recognition of my accomplishment graduating high school, it's a celebration of one of the most important meetings I had. The meeting I've had every single day I've had Linda in my life. It's a meeting where I am constantly reminded to never stop creating, no matter the limitations to my voice.

This is Not the End.

Special Thanks

LINDA

Mom, Dad, and Jack, you are my everything. Thank you for endlessly loving me, carrying me through the wild ride that high school was, and for never limiting me or my dreams. A special thanks to my mother for proposing the idea of this book in the first place—look what you've inspired! I couldn't do any of this without each of you. I love you so much.

Thank you to my extended family for supporting me in everything I do, and for treating Pudu as family. I am forever blessed to have you all in my life. Thank you to my great grandfather for showing me at a young age that any and all dreams are capable of becoming reality with hard work, regardless of age. Thank you to my grandfather, Chuck O'Connor, for continuing this lesson by living life with "unstoppable determination" and fearless love. Thank you to my parents and grandparents for instilling in me a strong sense of faith. To God, I am forever thankful.

Thank you to my friends Kelsey White and Sarah Somes for always being there for me, even when they didn't realize it. Thank you Camp Wawenock and the incredible people there who helped me find a home-away-from-home and always gave me a reason to be happy, even when school wasn't how I expected it to be.

Thank you to my teachers at Landmark Elementary Middle School for giving me an education that has allowed me to go confidently forth in the passion that I love—writing.

Thanks to everyone who made my high school experience something to always remember. I was fortunate to be born into the family I have—not just the members I share blood with, but all the people who have entered my life and pushed me onwards. This book is from my heart to yours.

Pudu

To Sarah McIntyre who is forever in my heart for the unending compassion and love she bestowed on me.

The friends I made, the laughs you shared with me, the parts of yourself you gifted me, the courage you gave me to embrace the weird world we live in.

The teachers who managed to impart in me years your of dedication to the acquisition and love of knowledge.

For my siblings who sometimes seem endless when I count, but contribute so much to the person I am just by being awesome and supportive. Especially Nehcopee and Jojo, you are so amazing and I can't wait to see what life brings for you.

To Aunty Abby for allowing me to see that I don't have to apologize for being unapologetically fabulous in the face of pain.

To my mother, as I grow and learn, I have come to recognize the beauty of what you created for us out of a world filled with malice. You are not only courageous, you have a heart of gold and I hope to be as strong a woman, as generous a person, as beautiful, and as God fearing as you are.

To Barack Obama, you made those years of high school easier, I will miss you.

TOGETHER

And It Begins would not be what it is today if it were not for the generosity of Tish O'Connor and Dana Levy. Your help has been invaluable. You cared for our memoir and us in a way we could not be more appreciative of. It is because of your hard work and assistance that we were able to take our manuscript and turn it into this book which we are so proud of.

Thank you to our GoFundMe supporters: Mary and Bob Fitzpatrick, Annie Baker, Beth Tauro, Chris and Dave Geithner, Anne Swayze, Muffy Antico, Michele Allen, Tod O'Connor, Anita Yawson, Gabrielle Coffman, Seema and Shuja Nawaz, Jennifer Rooney, Austin and Maureen O'Connor, Gemma Dorsey, Zahra Curtin, Linda and Chuck O'Connor, and Kelsey White. Your generosity was unlike anything we expected. Thank you for believing in us.

And thanks to you for reading this book and allowing us to share our stories. This is only the beginning.

FOLLOW US:

Linda's Social Media:
Twitter and Instagram: LindyFitzy
Blog (where you can read *Street Smart*):
www.dreamsarereachable.wordpress.com

Pudu's Social Media:
Instagram: bicolamoh

Made in the USA
Middletown, DE
08 April 2020